DOG SECRETS

(What your dog wishes you knew)

David Ryan PG Dip (CABC), CCAB

ISBN 978-1-4452-6159-1

DOG SECRETS
(What your dog wishes you knew)

Contents

Introduction
Why "Dog Secrets"?

For years dog trainers have tried to persuade us, the dog owning public, that there is something special about the ability to train dogs. They invoke some special method, mysticism or secret that makes them better than anyone else. Well, allow me to let you in to a secret: there are no "secrets". Anyone can learn the skills necessary to train a dog because dog training conforms to tried and tested scientifically proven principles. Unfortunately, these principles are frequently hidden away in specialist journals, crammed with technical terminology, so that the average dog owner has little chance of seeing them and much less of understanding how they apply in real life.

Television currently abounds with programmes fixing badly behaved dogs. I cringe at the lack of knowledge displayed by the so-called trainers or even worse, "behaviourists". The subject often comes up at puppy training classes, when I confess that I can't watch any more for fear of throwing things at the TV set in frustration. "But I love to watch," Ray told me, his mastiff lying on the floor allowing a pug to put her head in his mouth, "Seeing all those struggling dog owners makes me feel really superior!"

On one extreme you have scientists, who each have knowledge of their own specialist principles, publishing obscure papers from their research laboratories, and on the other you have practitioners, the tweedy lady with her local church hall dog club, the bloke who has, "always had dogs" or, even worse, the mystics with their "special" ways.

There are only a handful of people who have studied the science *and* had the opportunity to put it into practice on a daily basis - to find out what really works - to understand why it works - and when it won't. And that's the knowledge I'm about to give you - an insight into how the truly scientific principles apply in real life. The chance, like Ray, to be a superior dog trainer.

You'll be familiar with some of these principles but not with others, and that is the problem most trainers and self-styled behaviourists face. They've watched someone else training a dog and tried to imitate them. What they don't realise is that the person they were watching had watched someone else and they, in turn, had watched someone before that. Like the Victorian parlour game of Chinese Whispers, each time the method is repeated it changes ever so slightly until it bears no relation whatsoever to the original.

The more adept proponents of the techniques sometimes get it right but don't know why, so they make up some mystic words and call it a new way with dogs. Which is fine until it doesn't work and they have nothing to refer to. No basic knowledge to fall back on.

You will meet lots of people who say, "I don't need to know why. I've had dogs for years". Often this is followed by, "But she's never done that before!"

This book is about all the most up to date information on dog training in every-day language; how to go about it and the consequences of what we do. Incidentally, "most up to date" doesn't always mean "new"; some of these principles have been around for over a century! The fact that most dog owners and professional dog trainers are not aware of many of them illustrates the huge chasm in information that currently prevents us from understanding our dogs.

I'll be visiting studies of canine evolution and ethology (dog behaviour through the ages), of phylogenetics and ontogenetics (how canine genes make dogs what they are), of neurology (the brains behind it all), comparative psychology (training) and cognitive theory (learning), and I'll be applying them to real dogs; how they live, why they do what they do and how to change what you don't like.

There are no "secrets" to dog training. All the information is out there, but badly distilled. I've added it to over twenty-five years of experience of what works best and put it into the context of real life.

I have included some examples of the science in action and, as is usual, some of the names and the more identifiable details have been changed to save any blushes. However, I want to make it clear that no blame attaches to any person who is not able to understand their dog. People can only be at fault once they know what they are doing and, in every case I cite, they didn't know what to do. Nobody is born knowing how to train dogs, it has to be learned, and many of the people that come to me with problems have tried so many different "methods" their head is spinning. You can imagine how their dog is feeling.

The understanding of dogs is accelerating rapidly and some of this information might seem at odds with what you have learned before - what you believe to be unshakeable knowledge. That's not necessarily because it is new, it's because the information hasn't entered the public consciousness yet. When I started out training police dogs, over twenty-five years ago, the best publicly available information and, indeed, the Home Office Police

Dog Training Manual, was based on methods used in the First World War!

Dog trainers are a notoriously conservative lot, after all they are copying someone who copied someone who copied.... and that wasn't good enough for me. Things have improved a bit since then, but remarkably few people can translate the science into practice.

This is not about me teaching your dog, it is about showing you how to go about teaching any dog. I have my own style that works for me, and yours will be slightly different, but we will both apply the same principles. I can teach your dog to sit in two minutes, but it won't stop her chasing the cat. However, if you learn how to apply the theory, you can teach her to sit instead of chasing the cat, or jumping up at visitors or barking at the post delivery or any of a hundred other things you'd rather she didn't do.

The secret that your dog wishes you knew is how to transform the theories, collected by scientists of all disciplines, into real life dog training, and they aren't secrets, just things nobody has told you yet.

Chapter One

What is a Dog?

The Secret of How Dogs Came About

It seems an odd question to start a book about dog training, but lots of people have strange ideas about dogs. Some people think dogs are little people with fur coats and too many legs, whilst others think they are wolves, wild in nature and red in tooth and claw. As is often the case with these things, the truth lies somewhere in between.

Let's do an imaginary poll and ask who thinks dogs are the same as people, with the same needs and desires. Ah, yes, I thought so, a few people at the back, tentatively putting their hand up. And on a very basic anthropomorphic level, they're right. Dogs need food, drink and some sort of shelter from the elements to survive. A little more luxury, like clean water, a balanced diet, some protection from disease and parasites, warmth when it's cold, and support through the rough patches, and they can actually thrive. Beyond that, the similarity ends.

Dogs are a totally different species. They have a completely different perspective on the world and therefore a completely different way of relating to it. Their vision, hearing, smelling, tasting and feeling senses are all different to ours. Even their brain is set up differently; one whole eighth of it is devoted to what they smell!

They do not understand human language, and communicate with a combination of scent and body posture (yes, I know Tiddly-pops knows words like "walkies" and "din-dins", but read the previous paragraph to her and ask her how much she understood). They do not need or desire hats, dining tables, or books. They see no point in television, computers, or mobile phones. Given a choice they would not book two weeks in Torremolinos, a weekend at Brands Hatch or a night at the opera. They do not play squash, smoke, drink alcohol or take experience-enhancing substances as a form of recreation. They do not like a lie-in at weekends, ride motorcycles to look cool or stay up late chatting about where their relationship is going. They don't worry that their hair is going grey or whether their bum looks big. They don't scour the shops for the latest fashions or download the newest pop phenomenon to their iPod. They are obsessed with muck of all kinds and stick their noses in the most impolite places, then lick your face. They don't clean their teeth and their only nod in the direction of personal hygiene is a carelessly flung tongue. They are anybody's for a biscuit when the whim takes them and think urinating is a form of greeting.

In a survey of pet dog owners, it was reported that almost half the dogs showed aggressive behaviour towards people in more than one context. Over half consumed stones, their own, other dogs' or animals' faeces. Nearly all had soiled the house since they were supposedly housetrained and well over three-quarters engaged in some form of attention-seeking behaviour. Over half the people said their dog had an annoying habit (mostly barking and whining or lack of obedience) and over a quarter described at least one behaviour as a problem. Almost a third of the dogs had attempted to, or succeeded in, biting a person. And these are our normal pet dogs!

Dogs are decidedly *not* little people with too many legs and a fur coat.

What about the other end of the spectrum, though? Hands up everybody who thinks dogs are wolves. Ah, a few more this time! Probably because this was a popular theory some years back. It goes hand in hand with the vision of the "noble savage". Primeval man and his wolf, living side by side, each in perfect harmony with the other, battling against nature in the fight for survival, a loyal and enduring relationship evolving together. This myth spawned a brief bout of pet wolf or wolf/dog hybrid ownership, and continues to be perpetuated by dog trainers who like an air of mysticism. We can't all study wolves, because they don't live round here, but if a dog trainer knows the secrets of the wolf that makes them special. And it does. It gives them specialist knowledge of wolves. But are dogs wolves? We know what dogs are like, because they do live round here. What are wolves like?

A wolf is the ultimate all-round opportunist survivor. As a predator they have no equal in the animal world (except us, but we have helicopter gunships, so it's not really a fair comparison). They exist in places I couldn't more than visit without going home for a nice cup of tea, from scorching deserts to arctic tundra. They do it by being extremely adaptive.

Wolves have heads a fifth bigger than a dog of the same bodyweight, and when we match up the head size, the brain of a wolf is still a tenth bigger than the dog. A dog the same size as a wolf has a tiny head, containing a tiny brain, and Little Red Riding Hood's Grandma was right, dogs' teeth are about half the size of a comparable sized wolf. My, what big teeth they have! Even from that short description, dogs couldn't be wolves if they tried.

People who have kept wolves or dog/wolf hybrids as pets fall into two categories. The first is the man (it's never a woman) who bought a puppy from a bloke in a pub because it is, "A quarter full blood wolf. Straight up gov'nor. Behaves just like a dog, but it's got this wolf streak in it, see?" Yeah. Right. Somebody's Malamute fell in love with next door's German Shepherd.

In the second category are people who genuinely have tried to keep them as "domestic" animals (the word is in inverted commas because even the people who kept them did not regard them as domestic) including wolf parks and zoos. These are more interesting. For a start, if you don't hand-rear the wolf puppy before it is three weeks old, you can forget it. I'll look at what is often termed "socialisation" later, but for wolves to accept humans enough to be able to interact with them, they need people experience before three weeks old. You also have to continually work at the process. In one experiment, wolves, socialised to people from birth up to 14 weeks and then deprived of contact with them afterwards, at seven months old showed no signs of ever having seen people before! They were extremely fearful and, if approached, aggressive. Wolves don't interact like dogs.

The second problem is that they are extremely clever. They escape all but the most secure accommodation, making short work of bolts and latches. Occasional dogs learn that, but nearly all captive wolves do. The stories of wolf escapology are usually allied to stories of the inexplicable disappearance of pets and poultry.

What about teaching them things? Big brains make them clever, don't they? The best anyone has come up with is getting them to accept being walked on a lead. Hardly Crufts, is it? The problem is that you haven't got anything they want. They are independent - they don't want to please you. In fact, they don't care about you at all. They are very unlikely to do your bidding, even for a really nice biscuit. They'll wait until you're not looking, then take the biscuit and possibly some fingers. Wolf handlers walk very carefully and deliberately, so the wolf doesn't misunderstand their intentions. You touch them at their invitation only. Wolves don't want what dogs want.

But what about wolf behaviour? Dogs have the same behaviour as wolves, don't they? It depends on what you look at. What do people want from their dogs? Basically, the people in my puppy classes tell me they want them to come back when they are called, not to pull on the lead, and a bit of affection. No wolf has ever asked another wolf to come when it is called, not to pull on a lead or to give it a cuddle. How can we extrapolate asking a dog not to pull on a lead from anything a wolf does? Forget it, we can't.

Wolves only have the same behaviour as dogs in the way that a Formula 1 racing car has the same behaviour as a small family saloon. The basic parts are the same, but what they do is completely different.

Wolves can operate as a pack, an extended family unit. All members of the pack assist in the raising of the pups, from babysitting to regurgitating food carried back in their stomachs from the hunt. Dogs don't. Studies of feral dogs, living in the wild with no help from humans, reveal that although they form loose social groups, dogs do not communally look after pups born into their group. The puppy mortality rate is massive. About a sixth of the pups born make it to five months old and only one in twenty lives to be an adult in the group. No member of a social group, other than their mother, ever even visits young pups.

Neither do they hunt cooperatively. Despite an abundance of domestic livestock and wild deer, the dogs don't form a pack to hunt, preferring to scavenge individually instead. Yes, I know dogs chase sheep, but it isn't for food and it's not cooperative. They're playing a game, but you'll understand that later. Wolves don't behave like dogs.

But what about body language? Dogs have the same body language as wolves, don't they? Back to the Formula 1 racing car and the family saloon, I'm afraid. Wolves have marvellously expressive bodies and faces, allowing a huge range of subtle signals. Brows that wrinkle, independently mobile semaphore flag ears, eyes that go from bulging orbs to slits, lips that can snarl upwards or grin downwards, mouths that gape, with almost prehensile tongues, and not forgetting those teeth. Their bodies are lithe, squirming into the ground or standing erect with the hair on their necks and backs for added posturing. And last but far from least, their tails. Tails can be carried up, down, to the side, straight, curled over or under, and anywhere in between. They can move quickly or slowly, erratically or with an even beat, in any of those positions.

No dog, not even the ones we think look like wolves, can even begin to compete with that array of communication devices. Now think of a bloodhound, or a bulldog.

And I haven't mentioned the most important part yet, the environment. You see, giving off signals is alright, provided the receiver understands what you mean and gives you the correct response. Being born into a wolf pack gives them the ideal environment in which to practice giving and receiving meaningful signals, so they all understand each other, and continue to do so for the rest of their lives. It's like looking in a mirror.

Dogs, on the other hand, are born into, let's say, a Labrador family. All goes well as they learn the Labrador dialect (face not as expressive as a wolf, teeth too small, ears turned down, no eyebrow colour markings) and to be able to communicate with mum and brothers and sisters, that works fine. But at eight weeks old, when they enter the wider world, the social environment changes. They start to see all manner of strange looking dogs. Some have no tails, some have hair over their eyes, some have pricked ears and others have pendulous ones. What does it all mean? What do you do when you don't understand the language? You shout to try to make yourself understood, or alternatively, you say nothing. Many pet dogs actually learn *not* to try to communicate with other dogs, because it doesn't work. Certainly the smaller, subtler signals are lost, as dogs try bigger and bigger ones to make themselves understood. Dogs do not communicate like wolves.

But, but, but! Everybody knows dogs evolved from wolves, don't they? Everybody thinks they do, but, although it's close, it's not quite right. The missing part is the understanding that as dogs evolved, so did wolves. Neither is necessarily like the common ancestor.

If the wolf is the Formula 1 racing car and the dog is the modern family saloon, the common ancestor would be the early horseless carriage invented by Karl Benz. Neither of them is exactly like the original, although most of the parts are recognisable as having evolved from it.

Both modern wolves and dogs have evolved from a common ancestor. You will find a few stories of how this supposedly came about, but the only one that stands up to scrutiny is the "self-domestication" theory.

First of all, to understand the theory, you need a brief glimpse at evolutionary genetics. Stay with me, it's not as complicated as it sounds. (On the other hand, impress your workmates by telling them you've been reading up on evolutionary genetics.)

For genes and their bearers (in this case, dogs) to prosper, they only have to do one thing: reproduce. If the genes in dogs don't survive long enough to reproduce, they are lost to the next generation.

Genes can be viewed as instructions to an individual body on how to help that body survive and reproduce. They code for the building of it, for the survival of it and the reproduction that takes place. If the body survives, so do the genes. If the body reproduces, so do the genes. Replicas of the genes are passed on to the body's offspring, and those genes replicate again in the next generation. Successful genes don't intend to try to succeed, but rather they are successful and more numerous, *because* they succeed. If the genes benefit the animal, they will be passed on to many more animals, because the animal is successful in its environment.

Occasionally, genes make mistakes in replicating themselves. They make a slight difference to the body they are building. This difference can either benefit the body, or it can be detrimental. If it is detrimental, the body is unlikely to survive long enough to reproduce, and the "bad" genes will be lost to future generations. If the change (called a "genetic mutation") helps the body survive longer or reproduce more, which is often the same thing, more copies of it will be passed into the next generation.

Genes codify for everything about a body. Its shape, size, colour, behaviour, how fast it grows, and what diseases it will be susceptible to. Everything. A beneficial mutation, that is a change in the genes that helps the individual better at surviving or reproducing, is passed on, making that shape, size, colour or behaviour more prevalent in the group within which it reproduces.

Species tend to stay stable over long periods of time, usually because the circumstances in which they live (remember "survive and reproduce") remain relatively stable. This means that *any* mutation is likely to be detrimental and the offending genes don't make it into the next generation.

For example, if a giraffe was born with a genetic mutation that resulted in it having a shorter neck, it couldn't eat the tender leaves high up on the trees and so would die of starvation before it could reproduce, thus removing the mutation from the gene pool. The environmental geneticists will be crying in their beards now, but you get my drift, "bad" genes don't survive.

Occasionally something happens in the environment that makes it possible for genetic mutations to confer a benefit on an individual. This individual then has an advantage in survival and reproduction over the others in its group.

In the car world, the Karl Benz proto-car evolves a roof. People like staying dry and warm when they drive, so the roofless cars start to die out, all except a few that are good for racing in. Racing cars go faster without roofs, but they evolve into a different environment from the family saloon car. Each is good at what it does, but neither one is the proto-car, which was roofless *and* the family runabout. Family cars are no longer roofless. There are roofless cars about, but not in the same environment as family cars. The roof wasn't the only change, though. Lots of other changes accompanied it, comfortable upholstery, four seats and a boot for luggage, CD player, fluffy dice and so on, making it better and better in the "family saloon car" environment. Likewise the unroofed racing car got further and further from both the original *and* the family saloon; it excelled in its own "racing car" environment. Some features, like seatbelts and pneumatic tyres, were beneficial to both and evolved in the same direction.

As we can see now, one became a specialist, occupying a very precise area of motoring, whilst the other spread out, with lots of different kinds fulfilling the needs of all kinds of families.

The "hybrids" of the roof/no-roof cars, the convertibles, don't do either thing very well. They're not good racing cars, because they've got too many seats, and not good family cars because your children fall out when you go round corners.

Sometime before twelve thousand years ago the environment on earth changed. It changed because one of the inhabitants, humans, changed their habitat. They stopped being wandering hunters and gatherers and started to stay in one place. They settled down into villages and towns. This had a significant effect on the distribution of a particular food source: human waste. The by-products of human living opened a niche in the food market.

With a hunter-gatherer lifestyle, small bands of wandering people had discarded their waste as they went, a little here, a little there, and it was consequently scattered thinly over the terrain, making it difficult to find. Through the advent of permanent settlements, human waste not only grew in volume, because there were more people in one place, it was also concentrated in one area. Animal and fish bones, skin and offal, fruit rinds, spoiled leftovers, all the stuff we chucked away. Not an appetising diet for us, but relatively nutritious, all the same.

It would not have been too long before the proto dog/wolf realised that there was an opportunity to pick up an easy meal here. They would come to feed at the village dumps. This would be a very risky thing to do, as they themselves would be a good source of food for peckish humans. So they would sneak in under the cover of darkness, snatch a morsel and make off. This, however, is not a very energy efficient way to eat, and the calories consumed may be outweighed by the ones you expend darting in and running away again. You can only carry so much food away in your mouth.

This is the point at which our proto-dog/wolf began to diverge. The ones that were destined to be dogs stayed to eat and the progenitor of modern wolves left to pursue a more isolated life, away from humans.

In any group of individuals, there is small genetic variation. Some are slightly taller, some have different coloured hair, some are bolder and others are shyer. The wolves that were very shy could not subsist on what they could grab from the dump and run away with. If they weren't to starve, they had to hunt away from villages and people. As they stayed away from villages the only other wolves they came into contact with, and therefore had the opportunity to breed with, were the other shy ones. So the genes that produced the behaviour of staying away from people were successful so long as the wolves stayed away from people. They prospered in the right environment for them.

However, there were other genes, ones that conferred a benefit when the animal didn't run quite so soon or so far. Dogs (for that is what they are now becoming) didn't run away immediately they encountered people and they didn't stay away for as long. This behaviour, a reduction in what scientists call the "flight distance", conferred huge benefits.

Firstly, they eat for longer as the humans approach to within their defined "run away" distance, because it is much shorter than wolves'. If a wolf gets a whiff of a human half a mile away, it is gone. Feral dogs will tolerate the approach of humans to within yards, before moving away.

Secondly, running away costs energy. Wolves run over the next hill, and then probably some more, just to be sure. Feral dogs move a few feet away, just out of arms' reach, saving massively on the energy expended by a wolf.

Finally, wolves won't return for ages. They could be away for twenty-four hours, compared to a few seconds for feral dogs. Town pigeons have the same strategy, try them out sometime. Walk towards a feeding pigeon. It stays close to the food and just out of your reach. You need to make a scary noise or wave your arms about to make it take to the air, and even then it doesn't go far. It

25

has a high startle threshold and a tiny flight distance. Basically, it's not bothered by you and consequently it grows fat.

That, would you believe, is all you need to produce a tame animal from a wild one. In the first instance the dogs that stayed near the dumps began to breed with others that stayed near the dumps and in that population there were some that didn't run away as soon and for an even shorter distance. They ate, and therefore prospered, even more. The flight distance became less and less.

Of course this did not happen overnight. The first archaeological evidence for relatively permanent stone built human settlements are the Natufians, who lived in the Middle East about twelve thousand years ago. There is no great evidence of dog ownership there, simply because early dogs and wolves still looked the same. Is it a favourite puppy buried in the grave of the Natufian lady to accompany her to meet her maker or is it a savoury proto-wolf/dog pup snack for the afterlife? Is it a dog's tooth found in the Natufian living room or a trophy from a wolf/dog killed by the human occupants? We'll never know. What we do know is that the earliest settlements show no overwhelming evidence of dogs, but by seven thousand years ago they are everywhere. In evolutionary terms that is a veritable explosion of dogs into the new niche.

How do we know those later ones are dogs and not still the forebear type? Because they had changed shape by then. How had they changed shape? Back to genetics.

In 1959, Dmitry Belyaev of the Soviet Union's (now Russia) Institute of Cytology and Genetics in Novosibirsk, Siberia, began a breeding experiment with Silver Foxes; the work continues today. The silver fox is a wild animal that is kept caged for the fur industry. Being undomesticated they were handled with catching poles and very thick gloves. Consequently the mortality rate was high due to the stress of being caged and their proximity to humans. These foxes had been bred more or less at random for more than fifty years when Belyaev took over.

His idea was to breed only the tamer foxes to each other. He actively selected for a reduced flight distance, in the same way that the natural selective pressures operated on the proto-dogs at the village dumps. His selection criteria became more stringent as his stock became tamer, until the only foxes used for breeding were the ones that actively sought out human company. By the tenth generation almost a fifth of the foxes were approaching humans, wagging their tails and licking

27

people's hands. In less than forty generations, and within forty years, three-quarters of the foxes bred there behaved like dogs. There was no training going on, only selective breeding for reduced flight distance. This was intentional artificial selection, as opposed to the natural selection taking place around ancient human settlements, but what a phenomenally short time to go from wild to domestic!

And that's not all. Belyaev's foxes were less stressed, with a greater concentration of a "feel-good" chemical called serotonin in their brain. In short, they were happier. But the big breakthrough is yet to come. The tame foxes not only behaved like dogs in their interactions with humans, they also barked, had dropped ears, curly tails, and piebald coats. They looked like dogs, too! And all Belyaev had done was to select for reduced flight distance, or "tameness".

Charles Darwin called these extra effects "mysterious correlations", but we now know that when you change some parts of the genetic make-up it has effects on other parts, too. Known as "saltations", they are big leaps into different shapes, sizes and behaviours, and some scientists believe that this is how new species evolve.

Along with effects already outlined, there is an ontogenetic plasticity and the propensity to display paedomorphism. These mean that you can relatively easily get a wide range of shapes, sizes and behaviours, and that dogs display the juvenile characteristics of their forebears when they are adults.

Dogs seem to be permanently stuck in canine adolescence. In all species there seems to be three progressive types of hardwired genetic "sets" of behaviour: the neonatal (baby) behaviour, which is mostly crawling, suckling and crying; adult behaviour, which is mostly eating, reproducing and avoiding danger sufficiently to do the first two; and juvenile behaviour. Juvenile behaviours are a combination of the other two, and then some more. There is still some dependence on the adults, but a degree of independence not found in babies. Social behaviours are more complex as you need to be deferential to adults, but need to impress your mates. You start to find your own food, but still beg from mum and dad. Most of all, you have time to play. Play is the practise of behaviours (food gathering, protection or reproduction) that animals will need to perform as adults, but out of context. Juveniles perform them whilst they have spare time, so that when the chips are down they will be sufficiently good at them to succeed in their adult aims of surviving and reproducing. Have you ever noticed the similarities between the behaviour of human teenagers and dogs?

29

Canine paedomorphism is a result of breeding for a reduced flight distance. It provides behavioural systems of play, inhibition of aggression and, most importantly, the malleability of behavioural organisation. The adult behaviour of wolves is relatively fixed, but the adult behaviour systems of dogs are more like juvenile ones. Dogs are flexible; their behaviour can be manipulated. That's what makes them the pets we know and love.

Dogs tamed themselves sometime over seven thousand years ago. They entered the environmental niche supplied by the human development of agriculture. The first animals to be domesticated, domesticated themselves by exploiting our waste as a food source. By the way, I do mean *all* our waste products, so now we know why over half (that people admitted) the dogs in the pet dog survey consumed faeces. There is also a theory that this waste disposal system had benefits for the human population, too. If dogs eat your waste, it doesn't lie around to fester and ultimately cause disease. This has to be balanced against the waste that dogs leave behind, but, as it has been recycled once, it is proportionately less.

Dogs became tame because they developed a genetic predisposition not to run away from people. Now we're starting to get a firm understanding of what a dog is, let's look at the original dog as it was over seven thousand years ago and, for most of the world, still is now.

We often lose sight of the fact that most of the dogs in the world still live exactly as they originated. Our western-centric view of dogs is usually through the breed standards of the various Kennel Clubs, or the services they provide as pets, herders, guards, police, rescue and assistance dogs. These are only a tiny proportion of the world's population of dogs. The vast majority still make a living from hanging round human settlements. Go to any village where people scrape a living from the land, from New Guinea to Tibet, from Ethiopia to Bolivia, and you will find the original dog. They'll differ slightly from region to region, but not by much. Most of them will be about 20-25 pounds, shortish haired, tan coloured, maybe with patches of white and with slightly pointed muzzles, ears turned down at the top and slightly curled tails. They'll be somewhat bigger and with longer hair where the weather's colder as you move towards the poles or up into the mountains.

This is the original dog. It's not a breed, because nobody bred it. It evolved to look like it does because that's the best shape to fit into its environment. Likewise, it behaves in the way it does because that behaviour is the right shape for the environment. It is the ancestral form of all our dogs. The original dog evolved to fit a particular niche; they make a living from hanging round people, consuming readily available, low quality food. To do that successfully their bodies and behaviours developed in particular ways.

The wolf developed a big brain and big teeth because prey is difficult to catch and bigger brains and teeth helped them survive in their environment. The original dogs' environment propelled them in a different direction. Behaviours objectionable to humans would not be tolerated. Any dog behaving aggressively or, for example, stealing the chickens, would be driven away or killed, so original dogs tend to have low-level behaviours. They don't challenge people, they don't kill chickens or other livestock, they just exist in the background. Lots of the time you hardly know they are there. To eat poor quality but readily available food, they don't need big teeth or a big brain to catch it. Neither do they need to be very large or very small. Being too big means you consume too much food and also that you find it difficult to lose heat. Being too small means you have to eat very frequently and you find it difficult to conserve heat.

The original dog, like Goldilocks' chosen porridge, is just right. Now this really is human and dog living in perfect harmony. It is from this original dog that all our current dog breeds descend.

What? The scavenging mongrel scrabbling about in the dirt for its next meal doesn't inspire you? It doesn't seem as heroic as the courageous wolf, fending for itself, living off the land? Does it give you the impression that dogs are a degenerate form of wolf? Not quite as good? Not quite as pure? Not a real, proper animal? A bit of a sissy, dependent on handouts, not able to fend for itself? A poor quality canine?

But the original dog has something the wolf hasn't got - the characteristics of a juvenile. That means incredible possibilities for change. Incredible malleability in shape, size and behaviour. From the original dog have sprung dogs, ancient and modern, that can do every single thing a wolf can do, and do it better. Borzois see better than a wolf, Bloodhounds follow a trail with greater accuracy, Greyhounds run faster, Huskies run farther, Pit Bull Terriers are more persistent, Pointers are better stalkers, Terriers are better ratters, Labradors have gentler mouths. Stronger, taller, shorter, heavier, leaner, from hairless to hairball, from ghostly grey to spotted, from 10 ounces to four hundred and fifty times heavier at 286 pounds, from 3 inches at the shoulder to fourteen times taller at 42 inches. In every way, dogs exceed a wolf's capabilities. No wolf could ever guide a blind person, sniff out illegal drugs, pull a cart, or even sit on your knee. No other animal on earth can herd sheep like a Border Collie. Over a marathon distance, an artic sled dog is the fastest animal on the planet, on ice, pulling a sled! In human medicine, dogs can detect the presence of bladder cancer from a drop of urine and predict the onset of some types of epilepsy more reliably and in advance of any other method.

Nobody knows the exact figures, but there are probably a good deal less than a million wolves, of all types, left in the world. Add in all the other canids - coyotes, jackals, African hunting dogs, Argentinean maned wolves, dholes and the thirty-odd other less well know ones, and we might just make a grand total of fifty million individuals. There are that many pet dogs in the United States of America alone! Worldwide, dogs must number about five hundred million. There are a thousand dogs for every other canine on the planet. They are a fantastic evolutionary success story. So, I'll tell you what a dog is. A dog is the most incredible animal with which we share this earth.

Chapter Two
The Development of Breeds

The Secret of the Differences in Dogs

A guest at a Kensington dinner party points out the hosts' pet, curled up on the floor. "Aww, look at those eyes...What sort of dog is she?"

"Actually, she's very rare. We found her abandoned, living out the back of our holiday villa in Provence. She didn't chase the chickens and always turned up when we had dinner on the terrace, so we shared our scraps with her. She started to follow us around and we didn't know what she would do when we left, so we adopted her and brought her home."

"Oh, I see, she's a mongrel, then."

"No, no, no! We thought that at first, but we did some research on the internet and it turns out that dogs like this have been around since Roman times. She's a Marseilles Fishing Net Drag Hound. The fishermen use them to help bring in their nets. The pointy snout is the perfect shape for passing through the holes in the net and dragging it in, and the dropped ears prevent water getting inside. Of course she's short coated as it sheds water well, and the tan and white markings help the fishermen see them out of the corner of their eye, so they don't stand on their feet. The slightly curled tail wags vigorously to signal that she has hold of the net and is dragging it in. They do very well on a diet of fish guts. We've met a family who have another dog very similar, so we're going to start the first British Breed Club for them. We think the breed standard should be 20-25lbs."

And so starts another "breed". Creating a breed is easy. You take two dogs with a particular characteristic (or "no particular characteristic" in the case of the Marseilles Fishing Net Drag Hound, for which they will soon apply for Kennel Club registration and will be known to those in the know as a "Netty") and breed them together. From then on only dogs with that characteristic are used for breeding and the rest are excluded from the "breed", until you get the uniformity you desire.

Breeds are a modern construct, the last few hundred years has seen the biggest explosion of them, but how they developed from the original dogs goes back a bit further than that.

We know that the Romans, two thousand years ago, had separate dogs for hunting (split into sight and scent), herding, war, guarding and pets, and being fairly organised, wrote treatise on how to choose the right one for the job. The Egyptians left us pictures of greyhound types bred especially for coursing, between three and four thousand years ago.

But even before that it is likely that dogs had started to be bred selectively. In the previous chapter, looking at the development of the original dog, no human had yet interfered in their breeding process, and we don't quite need that yet. Originally, the dog evolved by being the right animal to fit into the ecological niche. It is a brilliant example of the theory of evolution by natural selection in practice.

But because niches aren't always identical, the dogs that evolve into them aren't exactly identical either. Even wolves vary in appearance in different habitats, hence the

Arabian wolf doesn't look like the Timber wolf because it has different selective pressures to contend with. I touched on these earlier, when describing the original dog. Depending on the village, the dogs may have evolved slightly differently.

If you'd been paying attention in Natural History class, you'd know that "Bergman's Rule" states (roughly) that the colder the habitat gets, the bigger the animals are, compared to their warm climate cousins. It goes for animals as diverse as sheep, bears and hares.

Basically the physics of a large body make it more efficient at retaining heat. The evolutionary principles hold firm: slightly bigger dogs and dogs with longer insulating hair would have survived and reproduced more in lower local temperatures when compared to thin coated or smaller specimens. The drift would be for larger, long coated dogs in cold climates. The limiting factor would be the food source; when it could no longer support bigger dogs the trend would level out.

Already, still within the boundaries of natural selection, we have local variation in populations of dogs. On the arid plains we have smallish smooth coated dogs and in the freezing highlands we have bigger, long coated dogs. But, being human, we can't leave anything alone...

Imagine the first human to befriend an original dog. Where the village meets the open plain, a young boy finishes his lunch before going back to work in the fields. A few local dogs are mooching around in the background, waiting to move in and vacuum up the crumbs when he leaves. But his bread was a bit hard today and he has left the crustiest bit. As he gets up, he sees three dogs looking at him out of the corner of their eyes. Just sitting, watching. One has a really curly tail, another is pure white, and the third is a bit fluffier than the others. He has a choice. Which dog does he throw the piece of bread to? Probably the one he likes the look of best. It doesn't really matter. He has just chosen "his" dog. He doesn't want anything from "his" dog, he just likes the look of it better than the other two. Tomorrow, he will be back. He may well favour "his" dog again.

We know that the mortality rate amongst original dogs is high, but they start breeding before they are one year old and breed twice a year to make up for it. Any advantage that one dog has over another will help that dog and its genes to survive and reproduce.

Three years later we return to the village and notice that almost all the dogs are white. There are none with fluffy coats or very curly tails.

There is one final way in which local populations of dogs can show variability, called the "Founder" effect. When any disaster, natural, biological, or even man-made, strikes a population of dogs, quite often one or two dogs survive. If an illness devastates the group of original dogs in one area, killing all but a few, when the population recovers it will resemble the few that survived the epidemic.

Likewise, after a tidal wave engulfs a tropical island, one pregnant bitch survives and with no competition for food she and her offspring thrive. Natural inbreeding, like the breed clubs set up today, produces dogs with the same characteristics. So, if the bitch happened to be particularly friendly towards people, by having a markedly reduced flight distance like one of Belyaev's foxes, the new local population of dogs would be mostly friendly towards people.

Combinations of these selective possibilities can account for a wide variation in the shape, size and behaviour of local populations of dogs. Add our "Favourite" effect to a "Bergman's Rule" and you get big white longhaired dogs. Add in our "Founder" effect and the big white longhaired dogs are friendly towards people. The opposite combination of effects, which is equally as likely, gets you a small shorthaired tricoloured dog that is aloof with strangers.

Either of these descriptions could be taken from a modern breed standard, and the amount of human effort that has gone in to producing such a dog hasn't gone beyond tossing one a piece of bread every lunchtime!

I told you creating a breed is easy.

In the development of modern dog breeds from the ancestral type we now have an animal that is acting and looking more and more familiar. We have changes in shape, colour and behaviour, and local populations that differ to the extent that they could be different breeds, if it had been entirely intentional. Most definitions of "breed" state that it is a group within a species that is domesticated, with characteristics that are intentionally selected and perpetuated. We're so conceited we don't call it a breed unless we created it!

It is important to reiterate at this stage, as we get more and more dog-like and less and less wolf-like, that the dog has all the genes necessary to produce a wolf. It is still the same species as a wolf, still able to breed and produce fertile offspring. It is those genetic possibilities that give us the next steps to modern breeds.

When you breed together two members of the same species that are as identical as you can get, they beget offspring that resemble the parents.

When you breed together two members of the same species that look or behave as differently as you can get, you don't just produce a combination of the two looks or behaviours, you create completely unimagined ones. The best way I can find to explain it, without using words like "phylogenetics", is to say that it looks like all the possible genes that these two parents carry are thrown into the pot and the offspring can inherit any proportion of any of them. The less alike the parents are, the more outlandish the offspring appear to be. Modern breeders are aware of the effect, but tend to shy away from it, because they don't know what they are going to produce.

Take a deep breath and consider this. We have a female Big White Longhaired dog that is Friendly towards people (BiWiLoF). We also have a male Small Tricoloured Shorthaired dog that is Aloof (SmaTSA). Here, each dog has only four characteristics, but in real life each dog has many, many, more.

If we mate the two dogs and the bitch produces eight pups, do we end up with four Biwilofs and four Smatsas? Of course not. We'd expect the characteristics get mixed up. We could get Big Tricoloured Longhaired Aloofs or

Small White Shorthaired Friendlies. But there is something even more complicated going on. Not only do we get a mixture of the characteristics obviously present in the parents, we also get characteristics that may not have been seen before. Ones that are possible within the genetic ancestry (that's where "phylogenetics" comes from) but not expressed in the present forms. It is like there is a huge genetic blueprint of all the possible outcomes for everything a gene can express carried within each individual dog. The more the parents differ, the more the blueprint reaches out.

Let's do a hypothetical experiment using just one characteristic: colour. Let's breed our tricoloured dog to a white bitch. We already agreed we won't just get four tricoloured and four white pups. But what we *can* get is incredible. Within the genetic possibilities are: solid black, white and brown; any solid shades of those colours including lemon, grey, red, golden, blue, silver and cream; any combination of those colours and any combination of shades of those colours including brindle, piebald, spotted, seal point, tricolour and harlequin. It won't happen every time, and quite often the resulting offspring will be relatively conservatively coloured, but just occasionally one or two different ones will show up.

People really like to have something different. If all the dogs in the village were black and white but "yours" was a blue merle, it would probably make you feel like throwing it a bit more bread. And it doesn't just happen with colour. It happens to every characteristic that genes have an influence over. Which is everything.

The general perception of Darwinian selection is that changes in shape and behaviour are slow processes. That to breed a dog with a two foot long tail, you start with one with a one foot long tail, then breed it to another with a one foot long tail and then their offspring with a one foot one inch tail to another with a one foot one inch tail and so on until you reach dogs with tails of the desired length. It doesn't happen like that. Anyone who has bred a litter of mongrels knows that some have longer tails than others. It is only when you breed dogs that are *alike* that you get a small range of characteristics. So there isn't much variation in a litter of Labradors because both parents were alike.

Breed a Biwilof to a Smatsa and the possibilities are amazing, not only in physical conformation, but also in behavioural conformation.

"Behavioural Conformation"? We've gone a bit technical there, haven't we? Well, not really, once you get your head around the idea.

Physical conformation is how the dog looks: the shape, size, colour that you see and how the genes operate on the dog's structure. Behavioural conformation is how the dog behaves: the activities you see the dog performing and how the genes operate on the dog's behaviour.

Back to the original dog again. I said earlier that the original dog selected itself to perform low-level behaviours, to be unobtrusive, and this is true. But the genetic possibilities of all our breeds (and of wolves) remain dormant in it.

Generally speaking, all canines are born with a genetic tendency to be able to perform particular patterns of behaviour. They have to be. They couldn't possibly learn the complex actions associated with food gathering, reproduction and avoiding danger with every generation.

These are the behaviour patterns that allowed the original proto-dog to survive and reproduce so successfully. Scientifically they are "motor patterns", genetically predetermined sections of behaviour that fit together like pieces of a jigsaw to make up the complete animal.

"Mum, we're hungry"

"I'm busy right now dear, go and catch yourself a rabbit."

"How do we catch rabbits, Mum?"

"Well, dear, first you have to put your nose down to the ground and sniff. When you smell "rabbit" you follow the scent on the ground until you smell "rabbit" in the air. You follow that until you see the tasty little morsels. Then you have to stalk them, so they don't bolt down the holes."

"Mum, Mum, what's "stalk" mean? And what does "sniff" mean?"

There are no schools to teach hunting, sex education or self defence and every pup has to know everything by the time they become sexually mature enough to start their own family, which is sometimes as young as seven months old. Teaching from scratch with every new generation would be horrendously difficult, so it has to be instinctive.

Food gathering motor patterns include things like tracking, searching, stalking, chasing, grabbing and killing prey. Mouse-pouncing, for example, is a predatory motor pattern that, once seen, is never mistaken for anything else. It involves a graceful leap into the air and a rigid downward stab with the forefeet onto the prey. It is seen in most dog breeds, wolves, coyotes, foxes and jackals. A variation is seen in cats, too, so either it is a very good motor pattern that independently developed relatively recently or it evolved before the canine and feline lineages split, about twenty million years ago!

The basic motor patterns are present in all canids and it is in the predatory motor patterns that we see huge variation in modern dog breeds.

You see, once you get a dog with "reduced" predatory behaviour but still the genes of its hunter ancestor, you get all sorts of possibilities. If you breed two dissimilar ones together you could get exaggerated behaviours in the pups, just like you can get exaggerated colours or shapes.

What if two original dogs produced seven ordinary, low-behaviour pups, but the eighth loved chasing small things. It accidentally inherited a big desire to chase prey. For starters it would get kicked out of the village for chasing chickens. But perhaps it chased the rabbits from the fields when the wheat was growing. Perhaps the young boy whose actual job that was, was pleased that a little dog helped him. Maybe he kept it on a piece of string to keep it away from the chickens and only let it off in the fields.

All right, I'll grant you there's a lot of "maybes" in there, but I'll give you another.

What if a few of the original dogs followed the people as they went off on a deer hunt, hoping to pick up the scraps afterwards? What if the ones with rather more inherited chase instinct joined in when the humans chased the deer over the cliff? You'd want to keep one of those, wouldn't you? Or...

What if hunting was bad and we only wounded an old buffalo that crawled off into the bushes? You don't want to follow a buffalo into the bushes, it might be annoyed. How valuable would it be to have a dog that, of its own accord, tracked the buffalo down so we knew exactly where it was? Or...

What if a small child took a puppy as a pet? Raised it. Pretended it was its own baby. Fed it. Grew up with it. The puppy would see the child as an excellent source of free nosh, without having to compete at the dump. It would follow the child everywhere, including on flock guarding duty. When the beasts of the night came to prey on the flock, the puppy would be scared and bark loudly (an inherited danger avoidance motor pattern), awaking the rest of the guarding party to protect the flock. Once it got over its fear, it might even join in chasing the predators away. What a dog that would be!

If you had a dog like any of those you might arrange a mating with your friend's dog that exhibited the same behaviour. Your dog might become famous. It might even be asked to mate with dogs from other villages, because it was such a good catcher of game or chaser of wolves.

Once you start mating dogs with similar behaviour or conformation together, you start to standardise, little by little. And that's how ancient dog breeds came about. Not overnight, but over hundreds of years, the fast runners were bred together, the baying hunters were bred together, the stoical shepherds' dogs were bred together. All it involves is identifying parts of the predatory hunting sequence or other inherited motor patterns, and exaggerating or reducing them. The dogs that don't fit the "breed standard" are culled, which can mean literally killing them, or expelling them back into the original dog melting pot.

So, breeds developed because they had a use. Particular aptitudes were enhanced by selective breeding even if that particular aptitude was just "being white" or even, in the case of our Marseilles Fishing Net Drag Hound "being in the right place at the right time"!

With the exception of the imaginary Netty, these are ancient breeds. We will look again at instinctive behaviour, but first we need to look at how the modern breeds came into existence.

All over the world there are examples of local variation. Almost everywhere that has sheep has its own sheep-guarding dog, but they look different. They all do the same job but vary slightly in appearance. Just look at the European ones: Anatolians, Pyrenees, Maremmas, Hellenic, South Russian, Akbash. Each was a distinctive population of roughly similar dogs doing exactly the same job, protecting sheep from predators. The behaviour was more or less the same and the dogs could have been interchangeable.

But, with a quick dip into human psychology, "our dogs are better than your dogs" in the same way that "our football team is better than your football team". They can be no better or worse, but locals identify with their dogs. They start to become symbols of parochial pride. "We love our dogs and will never allow them to be sullied by interbreeding with filthy outsiders!" And to ensure their purity, breeders start to exaggerate their characteristics. "Our dogs have slightly wrinklier noses than other dogs, so wrinkly noses are best". Artificial selection for wrinkly noses takes preference over working ability, which doesn't matter because they now live in town centre apartments.

Once a dog loses its working purpose and takes on another role, working ability becomes secondary to looks. Ah, the British Bulldog!

So we see the development of breed fancies. I'm not having a particular go at dog fanciers because it happens with almost every domestic or pet breed you can imagine, from geckos to goats. People seem to see the transmogrification of living animals as some sort of a challenge.

Some blame the explosion of hobby-dogs on Queen Victoria's love of all things canine but I think it was an inevitable conclusion of increased leisure time and income, pushed by human nature and some unscrupulous profiteering.

Today, the United Kingdom Kennel Club lists over 200 breeds eligible for registration, as does the American Kennel Club. The Verband für das Deutsche Hundewesen (German Kennel Club) lists over 250, and the Federation Cynologique Internationale (International Canine Federation) lists 331.

Not many of the registered specimens will be fit to perform their original purpose, either physically or behaviourally, but the original function of the breed gives us the best clue as to what, and how easily, an individual dog will learn. The start point for understanding how dogs learn and how best to teach them really is, "What sort of dog is that?

Chapter Three
What's in a "Breed"?

The Secret of Dog Genetics

The genetics of inherited behaviour. Sounds tough and dry. If I opened a book with that title, I'd expect to be reaching for the matchsticks to prop my eyelids open before long. But it's actually quite easy, once you get your head round the general principles.

We already know that genes control for the building of our dogs. They instruct our dog's body how to build itself. These genes are inherited from the parents, donated as a gift inside the sperm and the egg, like the instructions for a self-assembly wardrobe, but it builds itself and you don't have three bits of dowel, a sachet of glue, two screws and an odd shaped piece of wood left over.

The instructions are very precise. Have you ever made a table in woodwork class? Do you know how difficult it is to get all the legs the same length? Genes have it easy. They only have two basic commands - "grow for this long" and "grow that fast". All the dog's legs follow the same commands and end up exactly the same size. Indeed, each body part is instructed to grow "that" fast and for "this" long. It is the point at which they start and stop growing that is inherited from Mum and Dad. If Mum and Dad are Yorkshire Terriers, the point at which leg-growing starts and stops is considerably different than if they were Great Danes.

Different breeds have different onset and offset points for growth for different body parts. So, if we want a large portion of anything in our dog, the genes will have to code for early onset of growth of the part, grow it fast and stop growing it later than other breeds. It's easier than cutting bits from each leg in turn or sticking a book under one to try to stop the wobbling.

But you can't grow *behaviour* like that, can you? Actually, if it is inherited, that is exactly how it grows.

We already know that behaviours like hunting motor patterns are inherited and that genes code for them in the same way as for leg length. Before we look at the genetic growth of behaviours, let's go back to the predatory hunting sequence. I've mentioned it before and now it really comes into its own. It is instinctive behaviour that the dog has inherited.

Hunting behaviour is virtually hardwired into wild canids. To catch their lunch they have to go through a process of behaviours that have been honed by natural selection over millions of years. Let's look at a wild canid hunting prey.

At the risk of simplifying it too much it goes something like this:

It is lunchtime and you fancy a snack. First, like Mrs Beaton, you have to catch your hare. You can do that by *tracking*, which is following the trail left on the ground the last time a hare went past. Eventually, you will arrive at the hare but just before that, with a favourable wind, you will scent the presence of the hare on the air and you will switch to *searching*, scanning the air for the biggest concentration of scent. Closing in you will see the hare and at that point of contact you will have to *freeze*, to prevent being seen, and go into a *stalk*, creeping up on your prey or it will be gone in a flash. Once close enough, or if you are spotted, you will start the *chase*, running after the hare. Assuming you close it down you will be travelling at speed and will need to *grab* at it. This bite does not often kill the hare, so you then need a harder (or specialised) *kill-bite* to finish the job. Depending upon your size you may then need to *disrupt*, or tear open, the carcase so you can *eat*.

These are not *all* the hunting motor patterns, and it can be difficult to use single words to describe complicated behaviours, but they give us a flavour of the actions, and something to work with. I'm going to take "eat" out of the discussion, because it is not breed specific. All dogs eat.

Each of the other parts of this sequence stands alone as a motor pattern that the dog can perform independently. The desire to perform these behaviours is instinctive and the dog gets a boost of brain chemical reward for performing them. When our wild canid tracks, it doesn't do so because it thinks that there may be a meal at the end of it. It tracks because it gets feedback from its own brain that makes it feel good. It feels good to track. *What* it tracks is learned - track hares and you get fed, track cars and you won't - but tracking itself is just *enjoyable*. That goes for every other hunting motor pattern.

Now, because the motor patterns are inherited they can be increased or decreased through selective breeding, just like leg length. Our wild dog has to have just the right amount of each to balance out the whole sequence. If she liked tracking so much more than searching, she would track right up until she bumped into the hare, except that the hare would see her coming and have it away on its very long toes. The sequence would not be as efficient and the dog would not eat as frequently as dogs with the right balance, thus removing her from the gene pool.

Remember the original dog self-selected for reduced hunting motor patterns and then we selected ones with increased parts to perform certain functions?

Once we start to modify dogs they no longer have to answer to natural selection. We artificially disrupt their hunting behaviour for our purposes. So, whilst the wild dog is in perfect balance, our pets have hugely magnified or reduced desires to perform the hunting motor patterns. Selective breeding has enhanced some parts of the hunting sequence and reduced others, depending upon what we want the breed to do. They don't need the full complement of hunting motor patterns to stay in the gene pool because we feed them and decide on their breeding partners.

Let's have a look at some modern breeds and which parts of the predatory hunting sequence they were originally selected to perform in an exaggerated manner:

Tracking - Bloodhounds, Beagles, Bassett Hounds.

Searching - Spaniels, Labradors, Golden Retrievers.

Freezing – Pointers, Vizlas.

Stalking - Border Collies.

Chasing - Greyhounds, Salukis, Afghans.

Grabbing – Bulldog, Corgi, Heeler.

Kill-bite – almost all terriers (the "shake" that little Tiddles gives her fluffy toy is a specialised kill bite).

They often won't have just one exaggerated motor pattern, but different parts of the whole sequence will be heightened or lowered. Some will have the whole lot in varying degrees and parts of it will be virtually absent in other breeds.

Take a typical English Springer Spaniel. Their original function was to find small game birds on the ground and flush them into nets or for falcons. They therefore have some *tracking* ability, because if you get onto a scent it is likely to lead to a bird, considerable *searching* ability, because that is the main reason for working the dog, and considerable *chasing* ability, because you need the birds chased into the air. The breed profile changed slightly over the years and spaniels were later also used for collecting shot birds. This left them with no *grab* or *kill-bite*, because nobody wants their pheasants mangled and *disrupt* is absent for the same reason. Our typical English Springer Spaniel does not have *freeze* (point) or *stalk* because that would be detrimental to their work.

Don't forget that for each breed this was their original functional role, why the breed developed in the first place, not necessarily their current one.

So Greyhounds love to chase, but don't search. Labradors love to search, but often have no grab bite. Kill bite has been selectively lost from all but the smallest breeds. Who wants a large dog with a potentially life threatening motor pattern that it finds immensely enjoyable? Not me! A terrier performing the kill bite on my trouser leg is unpleasant enough thank you. I would not like a Great Dane performing one on my neck just for fun.

Why the differences in behaviour between breeds? Because their genes code for differences in the motor patterns associated with predatory behaviour.

The genes provide a blueprint for the dog's behaviour. They tell the brain which parts of the predatory sequence to grow. They give times for onset and offset for the possibility of the display of the behaviour. Read that last sentence again. There are two elements to the display of the behaviour: firstly the onset and offset times, and secondly it is just a possibility. The genes govern the parameters of what is possible.

You cannot develop the instinct to stalk in a greyhound because the genes do not code for the possibility. You cannot develop the instinct to freeze, like a pointer does, in a Corgi, because the genes that code for the freezing behaviour are switched off. To all intents and purposes, they do not exist within a Corgi. That is the first part to understand: genes set the boundaries.

The other consideration is the timings of onset and offset for any of the behaviours to be grown. Yes, the behaviours are grown in exactly the same way that a leg, a nose or a skull is grown. The onset/offset is a window of opportunity for the dog to display the behaviours. In the same way that bones won't grow to their full potential if the dog is deprived of food within the onset/offset of the growing period, the motor patterns will not grow to their full potential if they are not displayed during the onset/offset period.

Instinctive behaviour comes with brain patterns set up to perform it. All that needs to happen is for the behaviour to be performed during the time that the brain is receptive to it: the onset/offset period. This sets the brain up in the right configuration for the future.

Okay, it's getting a bit heavy again; time for an example: An extended American study worked with five different dog breeds, Basenjis, Cocker Spaniels, Shelties, Fox terriers and Beagles, comparing and contrasting their behaviour and that of their crossed offspring. One of the experiments involved testing retrieving behaviour, a combination of motor patterns expected to be found in the gun dog breeds, in this case represented by the Cocker Spaniel.

The test consisted of throwing a dumb bell and expecting the dog to pick it up and bring it back. They originally tested the Cocker Spaniels when they were nine weeks old. Three throws each day for three days, nine throws in total. Then the schedules got very busy and they had to put the experiment on hold for a while. They started testing again when the pups were thirty-two weeks old (that's eight months).

At thirty-two weeks old none of the pups of any breeds showed any interest in retrieving, except the Cocker Spaniel pups that had been tested at nine weeks old. The Cocker Spaniels that had not been tested earlier were no better or worse than the Basenjis, Shelties, Fox terriers and Beagles. The Cocker Spaniels that had the benefit of nine throws of a dumbbell when they were nine weeks old out-performed the lot of them. So what happened?

Cocker Spaniels have the genetic instinctive possibility to learn to retrieve (most dogs do), but it needs to be grown in the brain. The exact onset/offset of the growing period hasn't yet been pinned down, but it is certainly whilst they are young and probably specific to each individual. If Cocker Spaniels are allowed to display retrieving behaviour within the window of possibility, the right connections grow in the brain. If they don't, the connections are never made and the behaviour doesn't develop.

Of course, these dogs were laboratory animals and were kept in laboratory conditions most of the time, so they didn't get much chance to experience what we would call normal family pet life. Normal family pet Cocker Spaniels get to practice their retrieving skills inside the developmental period using tennis balls, socks, paper tissues, tea towels, slippers and any other toys they can get hold of.

It is the same with all the instinctive inherited motor patterns. Each breed is set up to learn particular actions. Performing those actions is rewarding in itself. It feels nice to track/search/chase/etc, if your brain is set up for it.

I keep getting asked, "How do I teach my dog to… (*fill in blank*)?". The secret is to ask, "What kind of dog have you got?"

Most dogs in the world are not pedigree, but most of the dogs in the western world that aren't, are descended from dogs that once were. Their forebears were once bred for an identifiable purpose. The chances are that, if your pet dog is not a pedigree, you probably know that she is a cross between a something and a something else. At the very least she will be a cross between something that itself was a cross between…

The point I'm trying to make is that most of our dogs are identifiable as being a product of breeding for a purpose. We *know* what our dog is, even if it is as vague as a "terrier cross lurcher".

The reason I'm labouring this point is that it is extremely important for understanding how our dog learns, because each breed is genetically prepared to learn different things differently.

The secret answer to "How do I teach my Labrador to retrieve?" is, "Wait until she brings you something and throw it again."

The answer to "How do I teach my Maremma to retrieve?" is "Why would you want a Maremma to retrieve?"

Labradors' brains are set up to make them deliriously happy when retrieving. Maremmas' brains aren't set up for retrieving at all. They just ain't bothered.

That is not to say that it is impossible to teach a Maremma to retrieve. It is possible to teach any dog anything that they are physically capable of, but it will be more difficult and the Maremma won't particularly enjoy it.

On the other hand, it will be very difficult to teach a Labrador *not* to pick things up and carry them about ("retrieving" breaks down into several motor patterns and the "bringing it back to me" part is influenced by the person). The action of holding things in her mouth is just so pleasurable!

Hang about a bit. Instinctive behaviour grows if the dog performs it at the right time, usually when it is a puppy, and it is deliriously happy when it performs these actions?

Yes. So, here's a test:

Question: What is the secret of, "How do I stop my collie chasing..."?

If you've been paying attention, you'll know the answer. The answer is that you can't. A collie's brain is wired to make chasing extremely enjoyable.

"But she won't come back for a biscuit...!" Eating a biscuit comes nowhere near the enjoyment a collie gets from chasing. What's the most exciting thing that you do? Skiing? Scuba diving? Free fall parachuting? Extreme ironing? Playing with your grandchildren?

Would you swap it for a biscuit? Neither would a collie.

Flash was about a year old when he was found, presumed dumped, on the roadside. He was scavenging road-kill to make ends meet, but quite happily trotted up to the farmer who found him and jumped into the back seat of his pick-up. As the farmer said, it was strange for a Border Collie that, although the fell-side all around him was teeming with sheep, he had made no attempt to chase them.

He was advertised as found, but nobody came forward, so he was duly adopted by Alice and Simon and settled in really well. Okay, he was a bit over-active, but as Simon said, "What do you expect from a year old collie?" Otherwise, he was so well behaved that no one could understand why he had been abandoned.

Until they took him fell walking. They knew he was good with people, other dogs and sheep, so he was rarely on a lead, and this day was no exception. Halfway up the fell, Alice and Simon cringed as a low-flying military aircraft zoomed overhead. As the noise died down Simon and

64

Alice stopped cowering and looked round to make sure Flash was alright.

Flash was more than alright, he was gone. He was coursing the aeroplane as it disappeared into the distance, like an express train. The jet receded to a tiny dot in the sky and still Flash had his eyes fixed firmly on it, galloping over the heather.

Even when Simon and Alice could no longer see the dot in the distance, Flash was still going after it like his life depended upon it. By now he was just a dot in the distance himself!

They both shouted for all they were worth, but to no avail. Flash just kept on running; over the horizon and gone. Alice and Simon were frantic. Six planes came over that morning and for five hours they called and searched, until they were exhausted.

The following afternoon Flash walked up to some picnickers in a car park almost ten miles from where he had last seen Alice and Simon. They rang the number on his collar and Simon picked him up shortly afterwards. Now we knew why Flash had turned up in the first place!

We had no history for Flash, but we examined his behaviour over a period of weeks. In the meantime he was never let off a long lead. What we found was that Flash just loved to chase aeroplanes. He wasn't really interested in chasing anything else; cats, rabbits, sheep didn't turn him on at all, although he *did* like to play with a ball.

But aeroplanes really tugged his rug. On hearing one in the distance (before we did) he would crouch on the ground and scan the horizon in the direction of the sound, his face alight with anticipation. We used that as a signal to take a tighter grip on the lead.

When he saw the plane he bolted after it until physically stopped or it left his view. We tried it in a walled garden and, as soon as the plane went out of sight over the wall, he stopped. On the open fell, when stopped by the long lead, he would crouch transfixed, staring at the diminishing plane.

It didn't matter what else he was doing when he heard one, he immediately stopped and went into "aeroplane mode". Sleeping, eating, playing, everything stopped for 'planes.

We didn't know why or even how, but in Flash's youth his desire to chase had been focussed on aeroplanes. Chasing them made him deliriously happy. My guess was that his environment had been restricted so that the *only* thing his brain could focus on getting enjoyment from chasing was aeroplanes. Perhaps he had been kept on a garden or a pen where the only moving things he saw were the 'planes overhead.

The inherited drive to chase was there and the only moving target was aeroplanes, so Flash's brain built itself around chasing aeroplanes for enjoyment. So much so that he ignored anything else to do it.

It was a long road to wean Flash from his aeroplane fixation, and we'll look at how playing appropriate games can help in later chapters, but suffice to say that now his favourite toy is a Frisbee, whizzed over his head to catch!

We now know why different breeds act differently but why do dogs of the same breed act differently? I'll show you. We're going to do an imagination experiment.

Inherited behaviour is determined by genetics, the same way that leg length is. Imagine one specimen of every breed of dog. Now line them up in order of each breed's average leg length, Great Danes, Irish Wolfhounds and Scottish Deerhounds on the right, tapering all the way down to Chihuahuas, Miniature Dachshunds and Yorkshire Terriers on the left. Deciding where each one should go might be tough sometimes. Does a Weimaraner go left or right of a Bloodhound? But in between the two extremes stand all the other dog breeds; a scale of leg length, determined by genetics, sloping from right to left.

Now think of the motor pattern that drives the need to chase. "Chase" behaviour exists on a continuum between breeds. Imagine again that you have one specimen of every breed of dog. You can line them up in order of how much chase behaviour each breed, on average, possesses.

On the right hand side, with a huge amount of innate chase behaviour, are the sight hounds: Greyhounds, Salukis, Afghans, Deerhounds, Borzois, Whippets and other like dogs. Differentiating between them might be tough. Does the Saluki go to the left or the right of the Afghan? Right down at the bottom end are the sheep guarding dogs and the hauling dogs: Maremmas, Pyreneans, St Bernards, Bernese and others. These are the dogs that do not get much, if any, of a kick from chasing.

In between these two extremes, somewhere along the line, is every other breed of dog. Where does yours fit? Border Collies to the right, Malamutes to the left, until we have a single continuous line of dogs in order of inherited chase behaviour by breed. The body shapes are all over the place, but the chase behaviour slopes from right to left, all neat and tidy.

But we know life's not all neat and tidy. These are the *averages* for each breed. Within each breed, there is also a range of inherited chase behaviour. Not all Boxers are born equal. Sure, the average Boxer has more inherited chase behaviour than the average Staffordshire Bull Terrier, but now we have to make another imaginary line. We need to line up all the Boxers that are alive today in order of their own chase behaviour. The ones with the most on the right, down to the ones with the least on the left. In front of them (because they are shorter) we line up all the living Staffies in order of *their* inherited chase motor pattern. Look what happened, the Boxer line starts higher up the scale than the Staffy line. It overlaps through the middle, but the Staffy line continues into the "can't be bothered" section, past where the Boxers end.

This means that although we can generalise and say that the average Boxer has more innate chase behaviour than the average Staffy, individual Staffies may have more than some individual Boxers. Just occasionally, you will get a Staffy with an abnormally high innate chase drive. Somewhere up in the Springer Spaniel range perhaps. Whenever breeding takes place, there is a scale of possibilities for "chase". Usually the resulting offspring are clustered around the centre of the average for that breed, but just occasionally, and exactly *because* there is a range of possibilities, one pops up with abnormally high or low innate chase drive.

Now then, time to boggle your mind. We have looked at the "chase" motor pattern and the variety both between breeds and within breeds. That diversity also exists for every other inherited behaviour. Not only the easily identifiable hunting ones, like tracking, freezing, searching, grabbing, and possessing, but also every other inherited predisposition, for example, "howling whilst running", "confidence", "the tendency to use aggression to resolve conflict" and "reactivity", or even just general activity levels. Like I said, some of these concepts are difficult to put into words, but anything that can be inherited exists on a continuum between and within breeds.

The good news is that dividing our dogs into breeds standardises behaviour most of the time. You know what you are going to get, within reasonable boundaries. Buy a Cavalier King Charles Spaniel and you know how much track, search, chase, confidence, aggression tendency, reactivity, etc, etc, you are going to get: roughly the same as all the other CKC Spaniels.

Sure, I know a Pyrenean Mountain dog that can't stop chasing: kids, ducks, cars. I know a Border Collie that lies about all day. Retrievers that crunch game. Terriers that befriend rats. Bloodhounds that can't find their way home. Cavalier King Charles Spaniels that hunt rabbits. Springer Spaniels that would rather sit on your knee. None of these has the "right" amount of inherited behaviour for the breed. But within breeds, and discounting the exceptional individuals at either ends of the scale, we have a rough idea of all the inherited behaviour your dog is likely to display.

Before we leave inherited behaviour I want to give you one last illustration of its importance.

Animal Behavior Enterprises was a Minnesotan company set up in the 1940s training animals to perform in the advertising business, TV, theme parks, and for anyone else that wanted it. One of their more famous enterprises was to train a racoon, for a small food reward, to pick up a coin, run across its cage and deposit it into a money bank, extolling the virtues of saving your money and good advertising for any bank.

They also trained a pig to do the same thing. Pigs are quite trainable, so it wasn't too difficult to train it to collect a token shaped like a coin, take it over to the "piggy bank" and drop it in, in exchange for a small food reward.

But then things started to go wrong. The racoon picked up the coin alright, but it didn't put it in the bank right away. It would rub it back and forth in its little paws, dipping it into the bank and removing it again, looking very miserly indeed. It reached the stage where the racoon, which had previously learned the task with ease, refused to let go of the coin, and just sat there rubbing it between its hands. The pig picked up the coin but, instead of placing it into the bank, dropped it onto the floor and pushed it around the pen.

Why would animals that had been properly trained to place a token into a slot to earn a food reward, prefer not to?

The answer lies in inherited behaviour and the rewarding properties of performing it. The pig and the racoon associated the performance of the act involving the token, with food. They each have inherited behaviour for dealing with the acquisition of food. Racoons hunt along riverbanks and collect crayfish from the shallows. Part of the process before eating is to break off the non-edible bits by washing them in their paws. This process is an inherited motor pattern associated with eating. "Letting go of your food item" is definitely *not* a motor pattern associated with eating. Any racoon that continually let go of its crayfish would probably starve.

For pigs, rooting in the earth is the motor pattern that leads to food. Again, "dropping the item out of sight" would not acquire a wild pig anything to eat.

The racoon and the pig were following their inherited programmes for acquiring food. All animals come with their brains pre-programmed to perform food-gathering

72

actions. These instinctive pathways are so strong that when they conflict with the training process they always eventually supersede them. Marian and Keller Breland, who ran ABE, encountered problems with cats, hamsters, cows, whales, chickens and rabbits, none of which performed as trained because they were trapped by strong instinctive behaviours. They named the phenomenon "instinctive drift", and it can be summarised as, "learned behaviour drifts toward instinctive behaviour". But what's all this got to do with dogs?

Well, anything a dog has been bred to do instinctively, it is biologically prepared to learn. All dogs come with a starter pack of genes. They instinctively know that lying by the fire, tickled tummy and sausages are nice. Added on to that is anything they have been bred to do.

"Prepared" in a learning theory sense has a special meaning and originates in the early experiments on classical conditioning. A dog is "prepared" to learn a particular behaviour if it comes to the table with its genes already set up to learn it.

Like the hand washing of the racoon or the rooting of the pig, your Beagle does not stick her nose to the floor and disappear into the distance because she was trained to do it. It is an instinctive behaviour. She gets a big brain chemical reward when she does it. In human terms it just feels nice. Really nice. With some dogs it is so nice that there is nothing they would rather do. They get the same brain chemical reward that ecstasy and cocaine users get when high, so you can imagine the addictive possibilities.

The people who were keen on banning foxhunting and thought that the hounds could be found a nice home as a pet were completely wrong. You just can't train a foxhound not to like tracking. They would go bonkers through frustration if you tried to make them into pets.

Understanding the parameters of breed specific behaviour means we can understand the needs of each individual dog. Controlling that inherited behaviour is the key to training any and every dog.

We will look at how to control our dog's needs later, but first, having decided that each dog is an individual, let's look at the learning theory that applies to all dog training.

Chapter Four

How Dogs Learn

The Secrets of a Teacher

The first part of how dogs learn is determined by their species and breed. You always, always, always, have to take that into to account when trying to teach them anything. Of course, each breed will have different learning preferences and each individual's preferences within that breed will differ slightly. If you want to teach a dog to herd sheep, don't buy an Akita. If you want a dog to lie in front of the fire for twenty-three hours a day, don't buy a Border Collie.

Surprisingly, after all that, there *are* general principles for how dogs learn that you can apply to all breeds. All breeds are certainly capable of learning the simple obedience exercises that allow for a balanced relationship. Let's start with the basics. All dogs can learn to sit when asked. Let's teach a dog to sit. You know how to do that already? Great, but do you know why it works or better, what to do when it doesn't work? Do you sometimes have to say, "sit" more than once or does she sit in some places better than others?

What do we use then, to teach a dog to sit? A lead? A loud voice? A hand to push down on her bottom? Nope, we use communication skills and an incentive. We need the dog to understand what we want and for the dog to want to do it too.

We need communication skills because this is a different species with which we are trying to communicate. It is not a furry little person with too many legs and a tail. Remember I said at the start that, "*good dog trainers are good communicators, whether they know it or not*"? Well now's your chance to become a good communicator.

Dogs aren't born understanding English or any other form of human expression. Why should dogs understand us when we don't have a common language? I know, we normally get by in the same way we speak to foreigners, slowly and loudly, and expect them to pick it up as they go along. That is the first mistake in trying to teach a dog

76

anything. If you wanted to teach an Italian to drive a car wouldn't you first learn a common language? If you wanted to teach a Greek to play cricket, wouldn't you need to be able to communicate?

The first thing we have to learn is to stop talking to our dog and start communicating with her, because if we want to teach a dog anything we first need a common language. Conversation gets in the way.

If I say, "Now then, there's a really good girl, I'd like to thank you for sitting just now, by giving you this biscuit." Which bit of the sentence does she learn? All of it? What if next time I say, "Well done puppy, that earns you another biscuit for sitting again"? How easy would it be for her to understand that? Dogs just don't do syntax, grammar, or even sentences. Single words are much easier to understand, that's why successful communicators use one word to mean one action. Now then, any ideas for what word could we use to mean, "Place your bum on the floor and don't move until I tell you, please"?
"Sit" seems fairly traditional.

This should not be confused with, "sit-down", which is impossible: "sit" meaning "place your bum on the floor", and "down" meaning, "lie flat on the floor".

Prospective police dog handlers are sometimes given a trained police dog to work with for a short time, to assess their potential. I once watched a prospective handler, Roger, give Belle, my police dog, the "sit-down" command. The poor dog sat, then lay down, then sat again, then kind of hovered between the two, bum on the floor and front legs see-sawing, with a strained expression on her face. She was trying her hardest to "sit-down". Roger actually meant 'sit', but he was conversing with Belle in a, "Would you like to sit down?" kind of way. The more he repeated, "Sit-down", the more confused Belle became and the more the assembled handlers giggled behind their hands, as I quietly fumed.

Consistency of use of the word is also very important. Start as you mean to go on. One word means one thing.

The next thing I want you to do is to forget about saying, "Sit" because we're going to teach our dog the action before we teach her the word. I know, it sounds strange, but trust me for a little while and it will all work out alright.

We also need an incentive for the dog to work for us. Why should she sit when we ask her to? Because we say so? Out of respect?

"*Because I say so*" and "*Respect*", are reasons I am given quite a lot, so let's examine them. We expect the dog to do as we say, when we say, without question and without payment of any kind. And we expect that to happen repeatedly. Isn't that slavery?

"But I feed her and keep her warm, cuddle her and take her for walks, and this is how she repays me? By not sitting when she is told?"

Would you not feed her and keep her warm, cuddle her and take her for walks anyway? When you got a dog didn't you intend to do these things? These things are a given. All dogs are entitled to them, for free! If you don't want to do these things, don't get a dog!

Actually, slavery might work to a degree, if you are sufficiently oppressive and the dog sufficiently submissive, but what kind of attitude do you think she will have towards you? Subservient, yes, but will she actually *want* to learn, want to please, rather than want to avoid the oppression? Will she work from enjoyment or from a desire to escape the consequences of not working? Which kind of dog would you rather have? A slave or a willing partner?

Anybody who said, "Slave" can leave now, and don't slam the door.

If you give a dog an incentive to perform an action for you it is the same as paying for work done. Tell me to go over there and sit down and I will tell you where to go. Tell me authoritatively, loudly and repeatedly, and you might eventually browbeat me into doing it, sullenly, if I can't get out of it. Tell me that I can have the hot Cumberland Sausage on the seat if I go over there and sit down and I'll do it with a smile on my face, quickly, and ask what you want me to do next. That's an incentive.

But we missed a bit there. To tell me to take the sausage from the seat, I have to understand what you say. Communication is therefore the key. How about another experiment?

You've got me, a room full of green chairs, but only one white one, and an unlimited supply of Cumberland Sausage (I *really* like Cumberland Sausage). How are you going to persuade me to sit on the white chair?

The slave driver would grab me by the scruff of the neck, march me across the room and throw me into the white chair, before eating the sausage in a smug self-congratulatory sort of way. In time, I get up and the slave driver sees another teaching opportunity, grabs me by the neck and throws me back towards the chair. In my headlong propulsion, I miss and hit a green chair instead, so I'm grabbed by the neck, lifted and dropped into the white one. I'm probably too stressed to learn anything right then, but over time I will eventually learn that, to avoid being grabbed and manhandled when the slave driver approaches me, I must sit in the white chair. Now, imagine how I feel about the whole situation, the room, the chairs and the slave driver. Good or not?

Run the exact same scenario, with the slave driver giving me a piece of sausage after I hit the white chair. Do I feel much better? Maybe a touch, but the whole affair is a bit nerve-racking. My first reaction would be, "Who are you grabbing, mate?" followed by, "Gerr-off!" and a bit of a struggle. I probably wouldn't notice the chair much and it would most likely put me off sausage for a while.

Let's try again. Let's get a dog trainer to persuade me to sit in the white chair. The dog trainer shows me a piece of sausage and beckons me across the room, turning slightly as we near the white chair, so my legs knock into it and I involuntarily sit down. The dog trainer says, "Right", and gives me a piece of sausage. They may have to do this a couple of times before I get the idea that sitting on the chair gets me a piece of sausage, but when the penny drops I run across the room and jump onto a chair. Unfortunately the chair is a green one. The trainer quietly says, "Wrong", obviously places the sausage in their pocket and turns their back on me for three seconds, before luring me back into the white chair and rewarding me with "Right" and sausage again.

I am actually learning several things here. That the behaviour required of me is "sitting on the white chair".

That "Right" means I have done the right thing and am going to get sausage. That "Wrong" means I have done the wrong thing and will not only miss the sausage, but also the opportunity to earn sausage for the next three seconds. On top of that I think that the dog trainer, the chairs and the whole situation is a pleasant experience and that I would probably like to play the game again!

This kind of training is called "lure and reward". We lure the dog into the behaviour that we want and reward her for being right. We added communication to improve understanding and also emphasise the difference between the right and wrong behaviour.

How do you teach a dog to sit? You take something the dog really likes and offer it above her head, reaching back until her bum hits the floor. As floor and bum make contact, you say, "Okay" and drop the treat into her mouth. Pretty soon she will be sitting *at* you. What to do if she tries to grab the treat? Say, "Ah," close your hand on it and turn your back for three seconds. Then start again.

What does our dog learn? That "sitting" is the required behaviour. That "Okay" means she has done the right thing and a treat is coming. That "Ah" means she has done the wrong thing and no treat will be arriving in the next three seconds. Finally, she learns that that you are in control of the treat and she must do what you want if she would like to earn it.

The words don't actually matter, they are just sounds that our dog is associating with consequences. It is called Classical Conditioning and the mechanisms for it were first proposed by Ivan Petrovich Pavlov way back in the 1890s, laying the foundations for a whole school of comparative psychologists and behaviourists.

At a basic level Pavlov's studies showed that if he rang a bell before feeding his laboratory dogs the bell alone took on the properties of the food and produced what he called the "conditional reflex" of salivation (he was originally collecting saliva from them, winning the Nobel Prize for medicine in 1904 for his research into the digestive system).

You cannot control the production of saliva. It is a reflex. You have no more control over your production of saliva than you do over your knee-jerk when the doctor hits it with a little hammer. It happens in response to particular stimuli. Don't worry about the terminology, a "stimulus" is some change in the environment that you detect: a puff of air, the smell of burning, the sound of a bell, whatever you notice, really.

What Pavlov did was to show that it was possible to pair two stimuli together so that a previously unconnected stimulus could produce the same reflex normally provoked by a more specific one. Remember, "Genetically prepared"? Well, the sight and smell of food is genetically prepared to bring about salivation. Sounding a bell is genetically *un*prepared to bring about salivation. It is not something that will occur naturally.

This was not a totally new concept, as Aristotle (over one and a half thousand years before Pavlov) knew that, when two things commonly occur together, the appearance of one will bring the other to mind. And we still find it intuitive: fish and chips, Mum and Dad, knife and fork, thunder and lightning, Ant and Dec and so on.

But Pavlov took it a step further. He showed that food provoked salivation, but if he paired a noise, such as a metronome or tuning fork, with the arrival of the food, eventually it alone would eventually elicit the salivation.

Note that scientists sometimes aren't that clever. Russian Pavlov called these "unconditional" when they occurred naturally and "conditional" when they had to be paired together before they worked. Somewhere along the way in the early days, "conditional" and "unconditional" were mistranslated into English as "conditioned" and "unconditioned", and have stuck with western psychology ever since. Scientists do not find this funny and pretend it never happened.

Let's look at it another way, because this is quite important...

For salivation to take place, certain cells in the brain must be excited. This doesn't mean they are having a great time, it's just a technical term to indicate that they are ready to fire. Once they are sufficiently excited, they fire and cause salivation to happen. These neurons are normally excited by other neurons that are in turn excited by the sight, sound, smell, taste or touch of food. You must have noticed the phenomenon whilst walking past a bakery, or a fish and chip shop?

As a kind of shorthand we can say that a representation of food in the brain, a food "idea", stimulates a set of "salivary" neurons to fire. It's good evolutionary logic. To survive and reproduce you need to eat. Having your saliva flowing when you need it makes perfect sense.

What Pavlov found was that if another set of neurons regularly fired at the same time as, or just before, the food "idea", eventually they too stimulated the salivary neurons to produce saliva. After several presentations of the noise and the food, the noise alone stimulates saliva production.

But, get this, *you can't help it!* It is a reflex. It happens because the "noise hearing" neurons and the "food idea" neurons have fired together so often, that the "noise hearing" ones have made their own connection to the "saliva producing" ones. Every time you hear the noise, you salivate! There is no choice in the matter. It's a reflex!

So, what do you think happens after several times of saying, "Okay" to a dog at the same time as feeding her a sausage? Yes, there is a join made, in her brain, between the noise of "Okay" and the idea of "sausage". In real terms we usually say that she understands that "Okay" means a sausage is arriving, but it is deeper than that. When we say the word, she actually thinks about sausage and the emotions that go with it. If the idea of sausage prompts positive emotions, then these too are associated with the word.

Right, two rules for this to work. First rule, what all good communicators need, be they teachers, comedians or politicians: timing. For effective classical conditioning to take place the two stimuli must be presented together. For practical purposes, get them within one second of each other. There are graphs that illustrate that the farther apart in time the conditioned ("Okay") and unconditioned (sausage) stimuli are, the more difficult it is to learn their association. For me it is obvious that the more things that happen between the word being spoken and the arrival of the food, the more difficult it is for a dog to associate the two together.

Second Rule: Predictability. Ant and Dec only go together in our minds because they are so frequently seen together on the screen. For classical conditioning to maintain its value, the conditioned stimulus ("Okay") must predict the unconditioned stimulus (sausage) every single time. Each time our dog hears "Okay" and no sausage arrives, the conditioning is degraded. Our dog learns that sometimes the sound does not predict the outcome and it weakens the reflexive response.

The good news is that once the connection is established, the one-second timing rule no longer applies. You can delay the sausage for a few seconds or even longer. The word still predicts the sausage, but because your dog is expecting the outcome, it holds the happy image until the sausage arrives. This helps people who are all fingers and thumbs, like me!

Once we have the "Ant and Dec" idea, each one stimulates the image of the other when seen alone. I bet when Ant does his shopping in the supermarket he is constantly asked, "Where's Dec?"

Our sitting dog also learns through classical conditioning that "Ah" means the loss of a sausage. No sausage arrives with "Ah", in fact, the sausage leaves!

This makes for extremely effective communication, because our dog *reflexively* knows that "Okay" means something good (sausage) and "Ah" means something bad (no sausage) and since they are attached to positive and negative emotions respectively, the words are instilled with huge significance.

Because we humans are such complex creatures, it is difficult to give examples that will resonate with all of us but, for me, the feeling of joy as an eleven-year-old on hearing the sound of the school bell signalling the end of the day goes somewhere towards demonstrating the power of classical conditioning. Actually, to this day if I hear a sound close enough to the tone of the school bell, I feel a little rush of joy inside, even before I register what it reminded me of. Other people have emotions brought to life by the smell of the perfume worn by their first date or the feel of sand in their toes.

Probably the starkest illustration of human classical conditioning comes from patients undergoing chemotherapy. People often feel nauseous due to the treatment, but the sickness is associated in their mind with a particular food as it happens at the time they eat it (often, ironically, the very food they are eating to try to stem the nausea). From then on, the particular food alone stimulates the feeling of nausea and in some cases even just the thought of it.

This kind of classical conditioning has also been used in aversion therapies for smokers and alcoholics, giving them drugs that make them feel nauseous (or even electric shocks!) when they smoke or drink. You will notice that our application is more positive than these last two examples.

It is on that level that classical conditioning works. It is not something that we consciously think about. After about twenty or so presentations, your dog will actually feel a positive emotion when you say, "Okay" and a negative one when you say, "Ah".

Oh, yes, I did say the words weren't important and the actual words you use aren't. You can use any words you like, but try to make them specific, so you don't confuse your dog by saying them at the wrong time, and you have to be consistent in word, tone and volume. Other words people have used are Yes/No (but we tend to over-use them and they lose meaning), or Yessssssssssss/ Noooooooooo, said in a funny voice (I could never get away with that), Right/Wrong (I find that strangely clinical). It doesn't really matter, it's up to you. You could use "banana" and "frogspawn" so long as you are consistent. Just bear in mind you will want to use them in public sometimes and you don't want to be yelling, "Armadillo" and "Pantaloons" across the common, do you?

But why do we need the words? In truth, for something as simple as "sit" we actually don't, we could just stay silent and let the sausage or lack of it convey the message, but it makes future communication that much easier and we are going to use them again, when we progress the "sit" into other training, so it is as well to get used to them from the start.

Now that we can tell our dog that she has done the right thing or the wrong thing, we can impress upon her that what she does is important. She starts to have input to the process.

This, scientifically, is "Operant" or "Instrumental" conditioning, and it isn't new either. If the Russians get the credit for classical conditioning, it seems only fair that the Americans get the credit for formulating the laws of operant conditioning, just after the 1900s, leading to the basic tenet that any action that is rewarded is more likely to be repeated and any action that is punished is more likely to be avoided.

To be fair, this isn't such a huge leap in imagination. Once you've reached the conclusion that dogs can associate two things that occur together, it pretty much follows on that they can associate what they do with what happens as a consequence of it.

In classical conditioning there was no need for our dog to do anything. She simply associated two things that take place together. "When the tin opener sounds, I get fed." or "When the lead rattles, we go for a walk." or "When the gate latch clicks, the post arrives." or, on an olfactory level, "When Grandma passes wind, everybody shouts at me." She could learn all that by sitting and watching. She had no input into the process at all.

In operant conditioning the dog learns that her actions have consequences and, depending upon whether these consequences favour or hinder her, she will make future choices as to whether she wishes to repeat each action. If she does something and a good consequence immediately follows, she is likely to repeat the behaviour. If something bad happens, she is less likely to do it again.

From the dog's point of view there are four possible outcomes and most so-called experts misunderstand them. In fact, it is a good way of judging how much your dog trainer knows.

I once read a newspaper article that said before you employ a gardener you should ask them how to prepare the soil to plant lavender, when to prune clematis and how to treat roses for mildew. If they didn't know, look for another gardener.

Well, this is my tip for employing dog trainers. Ask them to explain the differences between positive and negative reinforcement, and positive and negative punishment. If they can, they probably know what they are talking about (even if they don't know which way up your dog is). If they can't, they don't know what they are teaching your dog (or you).

Even though I'm not going to use all the outcomes to train, I'll give you all the definitions, then you know more than most dog trainers.

The proviso with these is that the *like* or *dislike* is always from the dog's point of view, and it is always immediate. It is no good trying to reward your dog by telling her, "Well done. You can stop up and watch Eastenders later." In the first place dogs can't associate delayed reward with the action they have just performed, remember the "timing" rule? And in the second place, whilst you enjoy Eastenders, it is a well known fact that dogs prefer football to soap TV.

I've seen some horrendously complicated versions of these definitions, but they are actually quite easy. No, really, honest! In each case the consequence happens whilst the dog performs the behaviour or, the same as in classical conditioning, immediately afterwards.

Positive reinforcement – something I like happens to me, which makes me want to repeat what I did.

Negative reinforcement – something I dislike goes away, which makes me want to repeat what I did.

Positive punishment – something I dislike happens to me, which makes me want to avoid what I did.

Negative punishment – something I like goes away, which makes me want to avoid what I did.

Again, with examples!

Positive reinforcement – something that she likes happens to her, which makes her want to repeat what she did. This is the most well known: a sausage for sitting. Every time she sits she gets a sausage, so she wants to sit again.

Negative reinforcement – something she dislikes goes away, which makes her want to repeat what she did. Tough one, this, as the dog has to be in a negative state to start with. If our dog is having her lead pulled upwards and her bum shoved downwards, when she sits, the pressure is released. The next time she is in the negative state of being shoved about, she may try to avoid it by sitting.

Positive punishment – something she dislikes happens to her, which makes her want to avoid what she did. If she continues to stand after being told to sit, whack her bottom (don't do it! It's just an example!) This makes her less likely to want to stand the next time she hears the "sit" word.

Negative punishment – something she likes goes away, which makes her want to avoid repeating what she did. Show her a piece of sausage. If she continues to stand after being told to sit, eat the sausage yourself (or put it back in your pocket). This makes her less likely to want to stand the next time she hears the "sit" word.

The clued-up amongst you will know which two we used in our example of training a dog (and me) to sit. You will also have worked out that positive reinforcement and negative punishment are opposite sides of the same coin. Both involve something nice. If she's good we give her the sausage, if she's not good we take it away.

Likewise, positive punishment and negative reinforcement both involve applying something unpleasant. In positive punishment it is applied when she is not good, in negative reinforcement it is taken away when she is good (you have to apply it so you can take it

94

away again). There is no great need to use these principles in general training, but we don't rule them out for dogs that are exhibiting problem behaviour.

Enough science! Back to real life dog training (phew!) Let's recap on teaching our dog to sit. We hold a piece of sausage over her head and when her bum hits the floor we say, "Okay" and drop the sausage into her mouth. If she does anything other than sitting, we say, "Ah", and take the sausage away. After several repetitions, the words become classically conditioned to the sausage or lack of it, and she operantly learns that plonking her bum on the floor gets her positively reinforced with sausage, but any other action is negatively punished by taking the sausage away. She feels happy when she gets the sausage, when she hears the word "Okay" and, through the magical combination of classical and operant conditioning, also when she sits.

Poetry in motion. You're applying "secret" principles in your dog training. Easy, isn't it?

But wait, let's up the ante. Let's really negatively punish her when she doesn't sit by taking away not only the sausage, not only the opportunity to earn the sausage, but also our attention. Say, "Ah", put the sausage in your pocket, turn around, look at the ceiling, fold your arms and don't speak any more. Now she feels really unhappy. Count to three in your head, turn around and start again.

This is "actively ignoring" your dog and it is a huge signal that she has done the wrong thing and is being denied her reward, the opportunity to earn it and probably the thing she values most, your attention. I bet within five goes you don't manage to turn away before she sits. That's how potent it is.

Up to now we've taught our dog to sit by using the hand signal that hovers above her head with the sausage as the request. We haven't used the word, "sit", at all. That's because we want the word to have importance. We only put it in once our dog has learned the action. We didn't use it earlier because we risk her ignoring it whilst she concentrates on the sausage. We don't want to teach her to ignore the word. From her point of view, what is important in the transaction that results in the sausage? Only her bum hitting the floor, not our waffling on!

Now we use the word, "sit" to predict the action of raising our be-sausaged hand. More classical conditioning. The word predicts the hand action and therefore has the same meaning. Very soon our dog picks up on the fact that the word and the hand action mean the same thing, because the "sound of the word" brain cells are joined to the "sight of the hand action" brain cells. Our dog's bum will start hitting the floor on the word, but before the hand goes up.

This is all very well, but you can't go around with pockets full of sausage all the time, can you? Of course not, nor do you need to. In fact, it gets better if you don't, but before we move on to more complicated training, a word about the sausage.

Now is probably a good time to get pedantic about the reinforcer/reward terminology. Not too difficult to understand, it goes something like this: A reinforcer is something that makes the behaviour more likely, a reward is something that the dog gets for performing an action. The very subtle difference is that the reinforcer operates on the behaviour and the reward operates on the dog. For most of our needs, it will be the same thing: the sausage reinforces the behaviour of sitting by making it more likely to occur again, and it also rewards the dog for expending the energy involved in the action of sitting. As I say, a bit pedantic, but scientists are like that and there might be one reading, so it's best you know.

Anyway, back in the real world, when you are training a new behaviour you really need to motivate your dog, so you need a reinforcer that has a high value. This is hard work, so we need something valuable to pay for it.

There is a test for whether you have a common cold or the 'flu' (unless you are a man, when it is *always* the 'flu', usually with complications, like rabies or beriberi). You are in bed feeling poorly and you see on TV that there is a philanthropist throwing money into the street. On screen you see there is a £50 note in your garden and if you can get up and collect it before the wind blows it away, it's yours. If you have a cold, you get up and go into the garden. If you actually have the 'flu' you stay in bed because the agony of getting up is not worth the £50.

It's a good test, and it is about motivation. How much motivation would you need to go into the garden *with* the 'flu'? If £50 is not enough, how about £500? £5,000? £5 million? I don't care how near death's door you are, you will eventually reach a price that motivates you to get out of bed and go into the garden.

If the money isn't reinforcing enough for you, how about a piece of paper with the cure for the 'flu' written on it?

It is the same principle with your dog. What will motivate your dog sufficiently to perform whatever training action we are asking for?

In most cases this will be a kind of food but just occasionally dogs prefer something breed specific, like a chase toy. Often, dogs that aren't particularly food motivated would rather chase a toy. If that is the case, find your dog's favourite toy and keep it for a reward just in training. Don't play with it at other times, as this will devalue it. Some of you will be making the classical association of "Okay" and tennis ball or tug-rope (or whatever).

If your dog prefers food, that is fine and easier to administer as you don't need to throw the ball and get it back each time you ask for a sit. But find your dog's favourite food and use that, not the ordinary stuff from her bowl. What? You don't know what she likes? For goodness sake, try some choices! Cheese, sausage, leftover chicken, or beef or liver; cat food (dried of course) or special (often expensive) doggy treats. Be imaginative. Try a few before teatime and wait until she goes cross-eyed with delight. That's the one to train with! Keep the pieces small, about half the size of your little fingernail for an average sized dog. The idea is to keep her coming back for more, not fill her up. It should be gone in a gulp and ready for the next.

These are Primary Reinforcers. A primary reinforcer is something that is reinforcing in its own right. The word "Okay" becomes a secondary reinforcer, conditioned by virtue of associating it with the primary reinforcer. The word, "Ah" becomes a secondary or conditioned negative punisher, because it is associated with having the possibility of a primary reinforcer removed.

There's one more type of communication that we need to address, before we move on.

We've asked our dog to sit, and she does, happily, because she wants to. We've taught her a word that signals she has done the right thing and will be rewarded for it (Okay), and another word that signals that she has done the wrong thing and will not be rewarded (Ah). We need one other form of communication. We need to be able to tell her that she is doing the right thing and should keep doing it.

Whilst this isn't too important with simple actions such as "sit", it becomes more so when we try advanced training, like walking on a loose lead. If you only had one word for telling her that she had done the right thing, you'd be walking down the road spouting, "Okay, okay, okay, okay", constantly showering sausage all over her. "Okay" tells her that she has done the right thing and can stop doing it because she is getting a reward. It signals the end of that discrete training episode (and you can then start another if you wish). For extended behaviours we need to provide feedback, otherwise how does she know she is doing the right thing? However, we also need her to keep performing the action.

Think about teaching a "stay". You say, "Stay" and walk away. The most likely way that she will break the stay is to come back to you when you walk away. How do you communicate to her that she must stay where she is? Remember, she doesn't understand the meaning of the word, "stay" as she does not understand English. Should you tell her off for coming back? Maybe yell, "Stay!" a bit louder? Think about it.

She doesn't want to stay whilst you walk away because she wants to be with you. She values your company. She wants to stay by your side to earn the reward. Aren't these the things we want to encourage in our pets? We will spend a lot of time trying to get her to come when called and walk close beside us, but for now we're going to tell her off for doing exactly that? I think not. Is this a failure to do as she is told (slavery again!) or a failure of our ability to communicate what we want her to do?

Should we say, "Ah" as a signal for non-reward? We could do. It is effectively communicating the consequences of coming back, but it is still a bit negative. Imagine telling our Italian driver only when they get it wrong but not saying anything when they get it right. We say, "Turn left" and they don't understand and carry straight on. "No!" we say, "Turn left". They switch the interior light on. "No! Turn left". They turn on the hazard warning lights. "No! Turn left". They make a U-turn. How many different manoeuvres would they have to try before getting it right?

Our dog is no different. She doesn't understand English either. Perhaps we could temper it with something more positive. Give her feedback when she is getting it right. Keep her emotions at the happy end of the scale. What we need is to be able to tell her that she is doing the right kind of thing and, if she keeps on doing it, she will eventually get the signal that she has done the right thing, and a reward.

How do we do that? We use feedback communication. Said in a nice, quiet, congratulatory tone of voice and, this time, the words actually don't matter. Say things like, "Good girl, well done, that's clever, good-good-good, what a clever girl." Words that can be drawn out into, "Goooooooood giiiirl, weeeellllll doooooone, whaaaaaat a cleeeeveeer giiiiiirl." This time it really is the tone that counts. Say it with a smile in your voice.

Let's go back a bit from the stay and revert to the "sit". She is now sitting, but expects to be rewarded with the sausage quite quickly. Don't reward her. Instead, give feedback communication telling her to keep sitting (don't repeat the word, "sit"). If she gets up say, "Ah" and take the sausage away. When she sits again, give more feedback. At the end of the feedback, joined seamlessly to it, give her an "Okay" and sausage. "Gooood Giiiirl. Cleeeeveer-Okay!" and treat.

The feedback is telling her, "You are doing the right thing and if you keep on doing it you will get the reward."

Technically it is also a secondary conditioned reinforcer, obtaining its reinforcing properties from associating it with the "Okay" and sausage.

Now we can really communicate! We have a word that says, "That was the right thing to do, you've earned a reward." A word that says, "That was wrong, no reward for that." and a series of words that say, "That's the right kind of thing. Keep doing that and eventually you will get a reward." We don't need any more than that!

So, "sit" training goes like this:

"Sit".

Dog sits.

"Good, girl, very good." Dog lifts bum off floor for a second.

"Ah".

She sits again.

"What a clever dog, good, good, Okay!" and treat with sausage.

Repeat as necessary, stretching out the feedback to keep her sitting for longer and longer before the reward.

"Stay" training goes the same way, as does walking on a loose lead training, and recall training. In fact, any kind of training follows the same pattern.

So far, we've looked at the mechanisms for learning, classical and operant conditioning, at the importance of secondary conditioners in communication, and at the value of the reinforcer, and we've only got as far as lifting a sausage above her head!

This is the very basic entry level, how to teach the start of anything, and you will quickly reach the stage where you need to progress, but progress to where, and how?

Chapter Five
Progressing Learning

The Secrets of Halls, Gamblers and Electric Collars

Millie was a model pupil. She was a ten-month-old Border Collie that had just passed her Kennel Club Good Citizen Scheme Bronze Award. Her Mum, Silvia, was extremely proud. She took Millie twice a week to the local church hall, where they met their friends and practised all the exercises. Everybody envied Silvia and her clever collie. They stopped having a "Star Pupil of the Week" award, because there had been only one winner for the past three months. Lots of the other dogs were told, "Why can't you be more like Millie?" So why was Silvia not happy?

Silvia had a guilty secret. Millie was indeed a star pupil in the church hall but she was a hooligan everywhere else. "I can't control her. She doesn't do a thing I say! She has a Jekyll and Hyde personality. When I say, "sit" at home she just laughs and runs away! It's got to the stage where she is so badly behaved, other than training classes, I can't take her anywhere with me."

In order to develop past the sausage-lifting stage, we need to understand the *process* of learning. We wouldn't expect to have a conversation with our dog, or draw some diagrams to explain about sitting, and for her to transfer that understanding to every situation in which we say, "sit", would we? Of course, dogs can't understand rationale and logic like that, but people expect dogs that learn to sit in a line of other dogs in a church hall to transfer that to all kinds of other situations. Why would they?

"Church Hall" training is when we all take our dogs along to the church hall, where the dog trainer lines us up and instructs us to make our dogs sit. On cue, we all yell, "sit" together and all the dogs sit.

Church Hall training is fine for teaching dogs to sit in a church hall, but it is very context specific. What was Millie learning? She learned that at a particular time, on a particular night, when Silvia wore particular clothes, in a

106

particular place, with particular other people and dogs present, she got a reward for sitting when Silvia asked her to. Was it any wonder she didn't sit at home? Not really, all the right things weren't there.

You wouldn't believe how many behaviour consultations start with, "The only place she does as she is told is training class". That's because the only place she has been trained to do as she is told is the training class. If we want to teach a dog to sit at home, we need to train her at home. In fact, we need to train her in every environment we expect her to sit.

Dogs go through distinct stages of learning and up to now we have been dealing with the very first part of stage one, which is just learning how to respond to something new. There are two more stages to look at yet.

Every new behaviour (sit, down, recall, somersault, anything-and-everything) passes through each of these phases and for the best learning to take place each one has to be mastered before moving on to the next.

I've described the first stage but didn't mention *where* we should start. Unfortunately for us, dogs have the attention span of a deficient goldfish, and puppies slightly less than that. They are extremely easily distracted from the learning task in hand. Therefore, the quickest way to acquire a new behaviour is to teach it in a place with no distractions at all.

The answer to, "My dog doesn't pay me any attention!" is that either the distractions with which you are competing are too great or the reinforcer on offer isn't of sufficiently high value. We are using the highest value reinforcer we can find and therefore we must also do all we can to eliminate distractions.

Distractions include: anything that moves (including another dog, cat, bird, child, butterfly...), anything new, anything edible, anything noisy, anything smelly. So, in a place with which our dog is very familiar, probably the living room, close the curtains, take the phone off the hook, switch off the telly, put the cat out, send the kids to their room, tell the neighbours not to call round, and teach. Just you and your dog. Short bouts of five to ten minutes are best and then take a break. At this stage there should be absolutely no distractions. Our dog is interested in the high value reinforcer and there is nothing to stop her from concentrating on acquiring it. Incidentally, if we are using food rewards, teach when she is hungry, before meals rather than just after will enhance the value of the food.

We quickly reach the second stage. The second stage is when the behaviour flows smoothly. We lure and she sits. Repeatedly. Every time. No messing about.

Whereas we started by using, "Okay" to signal the reward and, "Ah" to signal non-reward, a good indicator that we have moved into the second stage is that we don't need to use "Ah" any more because she sits every time. But we are still in the same place. We do not move out of the familiar place in either the first or second stages.

Because there are no distractions it is easier for our dog to concentrate on the parts of what she can observe that matter, so she picks it up very quickly.

Now she is fluent in sitting, it is time for the third stage. This is the stage that most pet dogs get stuck in. It is the stage in which our dog has to learn that the only thing that matters is the word "sit".

It doesn't matter whether we are in the kitchen or the car, wearing a trenchcoat or balancing on one leg; facing away from her or smell of garlic; whether we happily trill it or have a cold and snuffle it; whether I say it, you say it or your four year old niece says it; whether we've sausage in our hand or not. Nothing matters but the word "sit".

As you can well imagine, this is a huge phase. The good news is that we don't have to cover *all* the possible circumstances in which we might want our dog to sit, but the more we can cover, the better she will understand.

Distractions are our major enemy once again. How to introduce them? Gradually. Remember, almost anything can be a distraction, especially for puppies, so don't suddenly expect our pup to sit in the high street because she has mastered it in the kitchen.

Once our dog is fluent at sitting in the training place, introduce a distraction, open the curtains maybe, and watch our obedient pup suddenly forget how to sit. Don't worry, she hasn't actually forgotten, it's just that there was something more interesting than sitting, perhaps a bird flew past the window or she heard a cat three doors down! Drop back into the second stage, but aim for the previous level of response with the new level of distraction.

Not only will she improve again with practice, but it will be better than ever because now she can sit when there is some element of distraction. We need to introduce more distractions, always expecting a slight regression as we do so, and then practice past that point. In real life this means we take training out into the back garden, where it is quiet, then progress to the front garden, where there are people walking past, then onto quiet walks.

"This seems a lot of work, how much training should I be doing with her?"

How long's a piece of string? If she's paying attention and happy to play the learning game, keep going. The art is to recognise when she is just about to get fed up and stop. Every dog will vary, both between and within breeds, in the number of repetitions within training bouts and the number of training sessions they are prepared to participate in each day. One thing is for sure though, for simple behaviours like sitting, her daily total will be more than you or I can do!

But it's a long way between the sausage-tempting pose in the kitchen, to her skidding to a halt on your whispered "sit" as she charges after a rabbit. What do we need to get there?

Fortunately, the communication we already have in place helps enormously. Remember using "Okay", "Ah" and feedback communication? We did that for a very good reason. It helps our dogs to progress beyond sausage-lifting, making sausage almost redundant, and it works like this.

We have classical conditioning, in which we paired the, "Okay" and, "Ah" with the arrival or loss of a sausage. Classical conditioning works best when the association between the conditioned stimulus and the response are absolute. This means every single time we say the word "Okay" it must predict the arrival of a sausage. Not immediately, but eventually, like Ant coming on and introducing the programme, but you just know that Dec will be along in a minute.

We have operant conditioning, in which our dog learned that her actions had consequences, reinforced or punished by the words classically conditioned to the arrival or loss of the sausage. Paradoxically, operant conditioning works best intermittently.

Technically called "reinforcement schedules", they demonstrate that dogs are prepared to work harder if every action is *not* rewarded.

Once past the acquisition stage, where our dog has learned what behaviour is being reinforced, it is better not to reward every sit. The proportion of sits that are rewarded is called a reinforcement schedule. The most useful reinforcement schedule to dog trainers is called the Variable Ratio Schedule in which the dog has to perform an unknown (to her) number of responses before reinforcement arrives.

It is the same principle on which gambling relies. If a slot machine pays out in winnings 25% of what it takes, it means if you put a pound coin in, you should get 25p back each time. However, that wouldn't attract many punters would it? Instead, the machines pay out on a variable ratio schedule. Some mug or mugs thread pound coins in without any return, sometimes for ages, before someone comes along and wins the jackpot. On average, someone wins the £25 jackpot for every £100 inserted. Because of the nature of variable reinforcement we are prepared to risk working (slotting in hard earned cash) for nothing, just for the opportunity to win an unpredictable reward. In gamblers' terms, "I'll put another one in because this might be the time I win…"

Consequently, we reward our dog on the third sit, then on the fifth sit, then immediately after it, then the second after that, then the fourth, and so on. This has two remarkable effects. Firstly, the frustration of not earning a reward each time makes her try harder; we get better, quicker, more focussed sits. Secondly, the behaviour continues in the absence of the reinforcer. Our dog doesn't know if she is going to win a sausage after any particular sit, but the chances that she will are still enough to make her respond. And try this for size: the fewer responses we reinforce during training, the more she will continue to sit without sausage. It is almost like she is used to performing so many consecutive sits *without* sausage that she expects the more she performs, the nearer she gets to the "sausage-sit". The gambler would say, "I've put £80 in this machine up to now, it must be ready to pay out soon!"

And the extra bonus prize is that, if we provide feedback communication, our dog also knows that feedback is sometimes followed by "Okay"-and-sausage through the magic of secondary classical conditioning.

So what are we saying in practical terms? Behaviour actions will actually improve in the second and third Stages if we start to reinforce intermittently. We don't reward her for every sit. Give feedback, tell her what a good girl she is, but save the "Okay" sausage for only the best sits. Keep her guessing which one will earn the reward. Stretch out the rewards as far as we can, but just occasionally throw in a quick one.

Our dog is learning to sit quickly on asking, being rewarded less frequently, but being provided with feedback that she is going in the right direction and, if necessary, told when she has got it wrong. Eventually, the feedback itself is sufficient reward, as the sausage is almost totally phased out. Occasionally, just occasionally, if we reinforce with sausage, it will keep her razor-sharp. "Blimey! I got sausage for sitting again! I'll keep on doing that, then!" and like a gambler, she will keep coming back for more. Now you see why all the three types of communication were important.

Silvia's problem was that she thought Millie could transfer the learning from the church hall into every other circumstance, but the only time Silvia provided any reinforcement was in the church hall. If she sat when asked in the church hall, Millie knew that she had a good chance of eventually earning a piece of liver (Oh, yes, she was on a variable reinforcement schedule!) but she never got liver at home. In fact, there was never any training at home.

"We do that on Monday and Thursday nights, surely we don't need to do it at home as well?"

Actually, Silvia, you do.

We took a step back from Silvia's expectations of Millie's brilliance and started to train for ten minutes a couple times a day in the kitchen, then in the garden, then on walks, and eventually in the park, on the walks to the shops and picking the children up from school. Millie really was a quick learner and once Silvia understood the "secrets" Millie was as well behaved out of class as she was in the church hall.

At this point I'd like to return to the ways we can influence learning. You know, the ones I said you should ask your prospective dog trainer the differences between and, if they didn't know, tell them to take a hike? Remember positive and negative reinforcement and positive and negative punishment?

Well, it may have dawned on you that we've only used positive reinforcement and negative punishment. I did explain that negative reinforcement isn't much use because the dog has to be in a negative state to start with, but I didn't explain much about positive punishment. I suppose I should, on the one hand because you have a right to ask me (or tell me to take a hike), but also on the other hand because it is extremely interesting and generally very poorly understood.

Punishment, technically, is an aversive stimulus which, when applied, makes the performance of a behaviour less likely to be repeated. Or, in English, something I don't like that happens, making me not want to do *that* again!

If I put my hand in the fire it hurts so I don't put my hand in the fire again. Punishment works. Really, it works extremely well, but, as you'd expect, there are a few rules for it to be effective in dog training.

First off, it has to happen *at the time* of the behaviour. Delaying punishment makes it less and less effective. That is why it is no good telling your dog off for wetting the carpet two hours later. As in reinforcement, the best learning takes place at the time of the event. The fire burns me at the time I put my hand in, so it works.

The second rule is that it has to happen *every time* to be effective. If the punishment doesn't happen every time it becomes less and less effective. It's common sense really. If a young lad (hypothetically called David) only got caught and punished for scrumping apples from an orchard on his way home from school every twentieth time he did it, it wouldn't have much chance of stopping the behaviour. The fire hurts *every* time I put my hand in, so it works.

So now you see why punishment is starting to become a bit difficult to administer in dog training. We have to punish the behaviour *every time* it happens and *at the time* it happens. Quite difficult to arrange.

But the next rule is the doozy for me. The punishment has to be *aversive enough* to stop the behaviour. If young apple-scrumping David was grounded for one night as punishment, it probably wouldn't (didn't) stop the behaviour. However, if he had his legs cut off it might have (it would certainly have stopped him climbing trees, at least). The difficult part is that, like reinforcement, where our dogs' preferences dictate what they regard as a treat, their individual preferences also dictate what they find aversive.

Sandy was my explosives search dog and she *really* liked to search. She also had absolutely no fear of physical pain. She would fall from tall buildings, shake herself and go off searching again. She snapped off a canine tooth (one of the big ones at the front) by running full tilt into a storm drain cover, and the only way I knew was by the retort like a gunshot and the blood streaming from her mouth. She was not bothered in the slightest. She could have been beaten within an inch of her life and she wouldn't have been bothered. But she was sociable and loved company. Shutting her away, even for a short time, really upset her. For her, being ignored was a greater punishment than a beating would ever have been.

So, what's more aversive: being told you're going to miss Coronation Street or Test Match Special? It depends on your point of view. How, then, do we know what our dog thinks is sufficiently punishing to stop her?

We have a problem. If the punishment isn't severe enough, it doesn't work, but the severity is dictated by the dog's preferences. What can we do? How about we start off at a level that *we* think is quite bad and, if that doesn't work, crank it up a bit until it does? Nope, because animals get used to gradually increasing aversive stimuli. It's like the frog and the pan of water effect. If you put a frog into pan of very hot water it will jump straight out. If you put a frog into a pan of cold water and gradually warm it up, you'd not only be some kind of weird sadist, but you'd find that the frog could stand an even higher temperature. You can try a more benign version yourself the next time you have a bath. Get in the hottest bath you can stand and wait until it goes luke warm. Then turn the hot tap on and fill it up. You will be able to stand it hotter than you were originally.

That's why if you tap your puppy on the nose as a punishment you have to hit it harder and harder to get the same result. There is a "toughening-up" effect. This demonstrates to us that we only have one option for punishment to be effective and that is to come in at the most unpleasant intensity or above!

Up to now we had been talking about trying to punish a neutral behaviour. One that I had no reason to do, like putting my hand in the fire. But dogs don't do stuff without a reason and the usual reason is that they are being in some way reinforced for it.

They jump up because they get attention; they raid the bin because they get food from it; they chase rabbits because they find it extremely rewarding. What happens when we punish behaviour like that? They find another outlet for it. They bark instead of jumping up; they jump on the worktop instead of raiding the bin; they chase cars instead of rabbits. If the punishment stops and the dog hasn't found another outlet for the behaviour, she will go back to it. Behaviour that is being reinforced will find a way to surface through punishment.

So the next problem is that we have to find an alternative outlet for the punished behaviour. Not too difficult if the behaviour involves eating, because we feed our dog as an alternative, but what about chasing sheep? The dog wants to chase *something*, so if we are going to punish sheep-chasing we have to provide an opportunity to chase something else (like a tennis ball) or she will eventually go back to it again.

Any more snags with punishment then? Unfortunately, yes. Next is that too much or misunderstood punishment can lead to a state called "learned helplessness" in which the dog knows she is being punished but not how to avoid it. Basically she just sits there trying not to do anything, probably quivering like a nervous wreck.

Next (they don't half mount up!) is that punishment is not only associated with the behaviour, it is also associated with other stimuli that are present. That includes the place and the person doing the punishing. If that is you, then you become slightly aversive too!

And finally (at last!) punishment promotes aggression. How do you feel when you are told off? Resentful? Annoyed? Angry? Why do you think Traffic

Wardens are assaulted so often? Because they hand out punishments. Punish a dog often enough and sooner or later she may think not only about hitting back, but also about a pre-emptive strike.

Surprisingly, punishment can work. An electric collar is exactly what it says: a collar with a large battery and two electrodes that press into the dog's neck. It is operated by a remote control when you press a button. You can make it aversive enough because it turns up very high, causing a lot of pain. You can make it happen every time and at the time the behaviour occurs because you press the button. There is some risk of learned helplessness if you use it indiscriminately but if you're careful it should be okay, and you can provide another outlet for the behaviour. It is remote, so the dog is a long way off and shouldn't either associate the pain with, or direct the aggression towards, you (although she may direct the aggression towards *something*).

I just have one major concern. Do we have the right to electrocute our dogs because we are unable to communicate with them? I think not.

So what good is punishment? Well, nobody said "aversive" had to mean painful. I've already mentioned that social exclusion is very punishing for some dogs and a short time-out gives a clear message. Taste deterrents are good for dogs that chew, acting by punishing the behaviour of placing her mouth on the furniture, with a revolting taste.

My favourite at the moment is the "talking doormat". It is a mat with a pressure pad operated recording device. The idea is that you record your greeting on it, *"Hi, and welcome to the home of Sue and Dave"* and place it outside your front door, so that when people step on it they hear the greeting. A much better application is to record a message in a very loud shout, "GET OFF THE SOFA" and place it on the sofa when you go out. How many dogs know they aren't allowed on the sofa when you're there, but climb up as soon as you go out the room? The talking doormat does the punishment for you. The shock value alone should be aversive enough to keep her on the floor! On a smaller scale, the birthday cards on which you can record your own greeting may work for a variety of behaviours: "GET OUT OF THE BIN" as she flips the lid up could well flip her lid.

The bottom line for me is that if you can find a remote punisher that does not cause pain, make it consistent, contiguous and intense, use it sparingly, and give your dog another outlet for the behaviour, it *might* be worth considering.

Buzz is an Airedale terrier owned by George. George is retired, so they both take long walks on the moors. They get on tremendously well and George regarded Buzz as the perfect companion in all but one respect. Buzz loved rabbits. Not live ones; he quickly found out the little blighters are too quick for him, so doesn't bother chasing them any more. No, Buzz ate the dead ones he found on the moors. On a good day, he could pick up two or three in various stages of decomposition. It isn't that unusual. Remember that dogs evolved eating just such foods.

George is a tolerant sort of chap and didn't really mind Buzz having his tasty snacks, but he couldn't stand the mess Buzz made as the rabbits exited his system at the other end, particularly indoors. Eating putrefying rabbits gave Buzz the most horrendous diarrhoea.

Buzz knew he would be shouted at and, if George caught him, have the rabbit taken away but he just couldn't resist a nice decaying rabbit carcase. He used to scoop them up on the run and gallop in a wide circle back to George, chomping as he went. By the time he got back, the rabbit was swallowed and George couldn't shout at him because he *had* come back. Buzz's recall was excellent, but not until the rabbit had gone.

We thought about stuffing one with something bad tasting but this was a rotting rabbit carcase, how were we going to make it taste any worse?

Nevertheless, we set Buzz up. We caught a dead rabbit and placed it under a tree not far from home. We tied a piece of string to the carcase and led it up into the tree. On the other end of the string we loosely tied half a dozen baking trays (the ones for making cup cakes, made of light aluminium with rounded edges) and balanced them on a branch above the rabbit.

The trap set, George went home and collected Buzz like they were going for an ordinary walk. Approaching the tree Buzz picked up the scent of his favourite snack and away he went. He scooped up the bait and set off on his usual dash, about to munch on the rabbit. But this time he was followed by a huge crash as the trays fell out of the tree almost on top of him and then chased him across the moor. The faster he went the worse the noise was! Aaargh! Chased by the tray monster!

Buzz was so scared, halfway round his circle he dropped the rabbit and belted back to George who, trying to stifle his laughter, was calling, "Poor Buzz, what is the nasty rabbit doing to you, then? Come to Daddy and everything will be alright".

It was a perfect example of positive punishment. We had made a careful assessment of Buzz's temperament to make sure he could cope with the fright, it happened at exactly the right time, it didn't physically hurt Buzz, we only needed to do it once, it was aversive enough, it emanated from the behaviour itself, and it wasn't associated with George.

Buzz still picks up the scent of dead rabbits, but he approaches them very warily and it is easy for George to call him back and reward him with a treat for not eating them. Oh, and George's house smells a lot better these days.

Learning theory can be a bit of a slog, but, if you get this right, it makes training your dog a pleasure rather than a chore.

A final run through, to make sure you got it all.

- For any obedience training you need to be able to communicate what is the *right* behaviour, the *wrong* behaviour and the right *kind* of behaviour that will eventually lead to the reward.

- Start training in a place with no distractions, rewarding frequently with a high value reinforcer.

- Progress by gradually introducing distractions and phasing out the rewards; always give feedback, but reduce it to a minimum as she gets really good.
- If you have no alternative but to use a punisher, *think* about what you are doing.

Now you understand how your dog learns you can teach her anything you like, but even with all the learning theory in place, sometimes dogs still don't respond as expected.

Do you say, "Sit" and watch your dog wander off? Do you shout, "Come here!" and watch her disappear over the horizon? Are you dragged down the pavement, only stopping at convenient lampposts? Do you feed her best steak because she turns her nose up at Meaty Doggy-Chunks? Do you have an arrangement whereby she allows you to whistle as much as you like before she decides to come back? If you do, it is very likely that your dog has an interesting view of your relationship. In the next chapter we'll look at some important secrets. Who is actually in charge; is it you, or your dog?

Chapter Six

Relationships

The Secret of Living in Harmony

If men are from Mars and women from Venus, then I guess dogs must be from Pluto, the opposite end of the solar system and virtually nothing in common with the other two. Relationships are complicated at the best of times and have to be viewed from the perspective of the participants to have any meaning. Each person will want something different from their pet and often they don't actually realise the role their pet is performing for them.

Psychologists recognise that pets fulfil many functions for people and most of us will know someone who is accused of using their dog as a "child substitute". This can appear ludicrous when it is taken to extremes by dressing dogs up in human style clothes and constantly carrying them about but, viewed non-judgmentally, it can simply be an outlet for the affection that, for whatever reason, is currently not being expended upon a child.

What other emotional vacancy could a dog fill? Brother or sister, pal, peer, parent, playmate, partner, confidante, confessor, companion, fashion statement, ego boost, in fact, anything another person could provide, and then some. None of these are necessarily harmful. People have needs for outlets for their emotions and sometimes dogs provide them. In any case, before we cast the first stone, how many of us have enjoyed playing with our dog? Or poured our heart out to her after a bad day at work? Or felt proud that we have such a pretty/macho/clever dog? I know I have. And I've seen hard men cry over the death of their dogs. None of this is anything to be concerned about.

We each take something slightly different from the bond with our pets and, for that reason alone, the complex human emotional side of the relationship is beyond the scope of a dog training book. If you want to be analysed in that depth, go to a human psychologist, you probably need your head examined!

On that note, this is the chapter that separates the barking mad trainers from the knowledgeable. It clears away the cobwebs so we can tell fact from fiction. Old wives tales need dusted off to see if truth lies beneath them, new anecdotes need held up to the light to pass scrutiny. We're chucking the rubbish out of the dog-training attic. We'd better get a big skip.

Arrow was a police dog, or at least he was going to be a police dog. About twenty years ago, his owners handed him in to their local police force because they couldn't cope with him any more. He was a big fine looking German Shepherd and, at twenty-two months old, was towards the top end of the age range considered by the police. At that time police forces were still using methods based on dog training from the First World War, but there was some enlightenment dawning. Handlers were experimenting with newer, less "traditional" methods. Times have changed and, I'm glad to say, so have police training methods, however Arrow was to be a product of his own time.

He was duly assessed by the training staff, an appraisal that consisted of: "Will he chase a ball?" and, "Does he bark?" Arrow did both and was allocated to Brian, a novice police dog handler, on the first day of their training course. All went swimmingly well until on the second day they were paraded on the training ground for a beginner's lesson in walking to heel. Arrow was a little nonplussed as he was in a new situation with a bloke he had only met the previous day, so he was happy enough to sit next to Brian whilst the instructor went through what was going to happen.

They were going to step off together with Arrow walking, "...readily and cheerfully on the left side of the handler with its right shoulder close to the handler's left knee." Exactly as stated in the Home Office manual *Police Dogs Training and Care*. If correction was necessary, "...it should be given by means of a jerk with the lead loosened immediately."

On the command, "Heel!" Brian stepped off smartly and Arrow, not having read the Home Office manual, leapt sideways, dragging him off balance and into an undignified flap.

As Brian regained his composure the instructor advised, "Check him. Give him that short sharp jerk of the lead I showed you." Brian snapped the lead six inches to the right and back, which passed down to the check chain around Arrow's neck. Although his head jerked to the right, Arrow was determined to go to the left and redoubled his efforts.

"Check him again, harder."

Brian did, jerking Arrow halfway back into line. But then Arrow growled. A deep rumbling started somewhere in his lower bowel and resonated all the way up to his throat, where it stayed for a while, like thunder echoing in distant hills.

"Ho-ho!" said the instructor, "A dominant one! Check him again. Don't let him talk to you like that!"

Brian checked him again, "Bang!" tension on and off as Arrow's head cracked round to face him. Arrow was now rooted to the spot, feet planted squarely, every muscle in his body rigid with tension, hair bristling from the nape of his neck to his tail. Looking Brian straight in the eye, this time the growl was accompanied by a snarl that lodged in his throat, blowing frothy spittle as he showed every tooth he had.

"Ha-ha!" said the instructor, "Show him who's boss. Check him again."

But Brian didn't quite get the chance. As his hands moved the lead, Arrow's forefeet hit him in the chest. A frantic few seconds later, Arrow had been dragged from him and Brian was off to hospital with multiple puncture wounds to both arms, where he had fended off the bites aimed at his face.

Recuperating gave Brian the chance to think things over and he asked if he could still keep Arrow, as he thought they could make a go of it. He sat with Arrow in his kennel, made friends and, as soon as he was able, took him out to play ball. Everything looked good again, until they stood on the training ground and Brian increased the tension on Arrow's chain ever so slightly. That low rumble returned.

"We've got to do something about that dominance or he goes. You've got to show you're above him in the pack." The instructor decided.

Not one to give in easily, but also not believing that physical violence was the answer, Brian decided to use psychology.

Hands up those of you who have heard that the pack leader eats first?

Brian had, so, that teatime, he filled Arrow's food bowl and took it to his kennel. As he put the bowl on the floor he pushed Arrow away, got down on all fours and pretended to eat from it. Arrow didn't give any warnings this time, as he went straight for Brian's throat.

Brian was lucky that his instructor was passing and saw him on the floor, just in time to put his boot between Brian's face and Arrow's teeth, or it could have been much worse than it was. The boot rocked Arrow back just long enough for Brian to scramble out and slam the kennel door, skinned knees his only injury.

Why didn't that work? Everybody knows that dominant dogs are pack leaders and pack leaders eat first, don't they?

Ouch! Three myths in one sentence! I'm getting myth overload! This is exactly the kind of rubbish that has misguided people all over the country trying to get their dog to watch them eat a biscuit, to prove they're in charge. You don't need "secrets" to work out that's nonsense, just common sense.

Perhaps if Brian had understood Arrow a little better, he might have made him into a police dog. Arrow had ruled the roost at his old home. Everyone backed off him because he was so big and strong and he had *never* been checked by a chain. He was used to winning competitions and not used to deferring to anyone. The chain hurt and made him afraid of Brian, so he fought back. The food on the floor? Just plain crazy. Arrow had already bested Brian on the training ground, why should he defer anywhere else?

Arrow didn't become a police dog. He took a sideways move into private security, where he didn't have to walk nicely to heel and nobody asked him to do anything he didn't like.

What secrets didn't Brian know? Let's look at the concept of "dominance" first.

This reared its ugly head back in the 70's when it was used as a diagnosis for every badly behaved dog, but particularly those with aggression problems. It was a good cop-out for incompetent trainers, "It's not my fault. The dog's dominant".

It went something like this: "Ah, that dog pulls on a lead (or barks, bites, jumps up, won't come back, or any problem behaviour really) therefore it must be dominant". There was then a prescription that read: "Roll it over on its back and hold it down" (sometimes known as the "alpha roll"), "stare it into submission until it turns its head away" and "hold its muzzle closed."

These weird and wonderful wrestling moves were supposedly things that people had seen wolves do to other wolves to manifest their "dominance". The advice was not only misguided (how many times do I have to say, "Dogs aren't wolves"?), it was positively dangerous. Trying to hold down a fearfully aggressive dog will get you bitten! Time to expose the myths.

No wolf ever rolled another wolf over onto its back and held it there. You will see wolves roll over onto their backs in the presence of another wolf, but the crucial part is that they roll over voluntarily. It is an inherited social motor pattern that wolves use to show they mean no harm when they feel threatened. Think of the mind-set of the wolf that rolls over. It is fearful and wants to appease the threat. Think of the mind-set of the dog that is grabbed and rolled over. She is puzzled, to say the least. Can we get from puzzled to threatened? Do we want our dog to feel threatened? In any case, does either of these internal states help us control our dog? I don't think so.

Like most motor patterns, "rolling over" exists to a greater or lesser degree in most dogs. Some dogs will roll on their backs at the least perception of a threat. Conversely, I couldn't conceivably threaten my dog enough to make her roll over voluntarily. Nor would I want to.

"Stare it into submission" depends upon what the dog has learned. Some dogs will regard fixed eye contact as a threat because they have learned through classical conditioning that it predicts a telling off (or worse), especially with the frowning face that usually accompanies it. What will your dog do? Look away? Walk away? How will that help you control her?

I teach my dogs to look at me to say "please", to ask permission to do anything. If I try to "stare them into submission", they stare right back!

"Hold its muzzle closed". Wolves hold other wolves' muzzles in their jaws, not their hands. Any takers? All you are doing by grasping a dog's mouth in your hand is performing an action your dog doesn't like. It is straight punishment. What is it punishing? Well, your proximity for a start! Do I want to be close to someone who holds my mouth shut? Probably not.

I said earlier that the crucial part was the wolf rolling over voluntarily. That's the clue to the concept of dominance.

Dominance is not a heritable characteristic for a dog any more than it is inbuilt in a person. You wouldn't consider saying, "That is a genetically dominant person", would you? Dogs aren't born dominant, any more than they are born musical or able to ride a bike. Dominance is a consequence of a relationship, a product of learning that remains fluid within that relationship. And, get this: *it can only be conferred*, not earned. Someone else can only be dominant if you allow it to happen. You allow it by submitting to their wishes.

If our dog appears to be dominant in certain circumstances, it is because we allow her to be. We can rescind that permission at any time, without recourse to "alpha rolls" and the like.

Every relationship is a series of compromises. In choosing a restaurant, my wife Sue is dominant over me. In choosing the wine when we get there, I am dominant over Sue. This arises because I'm not a very good judge of places to eat and am prepared to follow her excellent lead, but I do care deeply about the wine I drink and she yields to my judgement in that. Either of these can only happen because the other submits.

"I want to go to Francorelli's"

"No, they're rubbish, we should go to Albertorolli's, they're good."

"Okay then, you win, we'll go there".

So, instead of examining dominance, we should be examining submission. Why do we submit in any competition? Well, humans are considerably more complex, but on the dog level there are some simple guidelines.

Imagine we are two dogs sitting facing each other, six feet apart. Exactly halfway between us is a piece of steak. Which of us gets the steak and why?

If we both lunge for it there will be a big fight but, before that, each of us have two considerations to take into account (stay tuned fight-lovers, it could still happen!)

Firstly, the value of the resource. Remember dogs will work harder for a valuable treat? This can be calculated as, "How hungry am I?" And "How much do I like steak?" If I value it less than you do, I will defer and you will be dominant *in this situation*.

Secondly, our assessment of each other. This can be considered as our personal history of competition, "Do you often defer to me?" If you do, the value of the steak being equal, you are more likely to defer to me again. Also, "Do others often defer to me?" If others constantly defer to me, I am used to others backing down and will expect you to do the same. If there is no previous history, I take what clues I can from your appearance and demeanour (perhaps shown by your teeth).

So, what are the possible outcomes?

1. If we both value the steak highly and we are both used to winning competitions, we will both go for it and there will be a big fight. We both end up bloodied and battered, probably with a bit of the steak each. Neither of us backs down, neither of us defers, and consequently neither of us is dominant.

2. I always win *any* competition with you, so you think there is no point in trying and walk away, leaving me

the steak. You admit defeat therefore I am dominant in this situation.

3. Even though I always win any competition with you, I am not hungry, having just eaten my fill of Cumberland sausage, and walk away, leaving you the steak. I yield and therefore you are dominant.

4. The roles can be reversed for number 2.

5. The roles can be reversed for number 3.

Notice anything there? From five possible outcomes the only scenario with aggression was the one where there was no dominance. Anything else? The dominance was conferred by the other party walking away from something they didn't want, not by fighting for it.

In real life, it is not always this cut and dried. Often, there will be a combination of effects that results in a bit of posturing, hair raising and chest-puffing before one or other decides it isn't worth the hassle.

This is just one example of a single interaction. Our dogs are constantly involved in countless similarly small events every day. Because of the huge number of interactions constantly taking place we can be assured that no dog is ever totally dominant over any other dog (or person). Each situation will have different value for each participant, especially so when they are different species, like humans and dogs.

Studies of pet dogs living in groups show that there is rarely a nice linear hierarchy, where:

- Alfie dominates Ben, Cindy, Dougal & Ethel;
- Ben is dominated by Alfie, but dominates Cindy, Dougal & Ethel;
- Cindy is dominated by Alfie & Ben, but dominates Dougal & Ethel;
- and so on right down to Ethel on the bottom rung.

Observations show group living to be an extremely complex web of interactions where preferences dictate the value of a resource and the desire to defend it (kind of like the Big Brother House for dogs).

For example, if Ethel had arthritis and liked to sit by the fire, none of the other fitter and stronger dogs would dare try to move her because warmth means a lot to her. Ben may be very quick and always beat the others to food dropped on the floor, so the others stop trying to get there first. Cindy is very shy and likes to sit on Mum's knee. Dougal may be first to lead the charge at next-door's cat.

Therefore, Ethel is in charge of sleeping places, Ben is in charge of food, Cindy is in charge of access to Mum and Dougal is in charge of hunting! Very often, none of the dogs in a group will able, or try, to monopolise all the resources.

Now, pack leadership seems more democratic doesn't it? If sufficient others defer to you in sufficient circumstances, you are promoted to pack leader. Ah, but that scotches the next myth: "Everyone must strive be pack leader and pack leader rules by dominating". Tosh. We already know that dogs don't truly pack from Chapter One. Wolf packs work together in concert to a common end. Not only Mum, but Dad, aunts and uncles regurgitate food for pups. Older brothers and sisters baby-sit.

By the way, regurgitation raises an interesting point. If the adult male "alpha" wolf comes back from the hunt and regurgitates for the pups, do they think they are dominant because they are eating without seeing him eat, or does he have to eat a biscuit first? I hope that debunks the final myth. You don't have to eat first to be in control of the food.

The "alpha" theory of dominance competition was first proposed by wolf experts who were observing packs of captured wolves thrown together in zoo-parks. These wolves had no relationship with each other and were provided with only limited resources within a restricted area. It is little wonder their stress levels went through the roof and they fought each other at the drop of a bone.

Natural wolf packs consist of a family. The breeding pair look after their offspring until they grow old enough to strike out on their own and find a partner. There is consequently a great deal of cooperation and little conflict. Even the wolf experts who devised the "alpha" dominance model have since renounced it as unsound. But we still have dog trainers using it.

Think about it. Trainers are using a theory that was mistakenly, but is no longer, applied to a type of canine that does not behave in the same way as domestic dogs. How wrong can it get?

Dogs don't actually pack in the cooperative way wolves do, but they do congregate in groups around sources of food, that's how the original dog evolved. That does not imply any kind of cooperation, in fact each dog works to maximise their own benefits regardless of others in the group. The only area in which there was any benefit for free roaming feral dogs living in groups was in defence of their territory. Lots of dogs barking at the same time were more effective at keeping others away than a few dogs barking. Anthropomorphists might suggest that the dogs got together and decided to form a big group to defend their food source (before rushing into the village to bark out a warning that little Jimmy had fallen down the old mine shaft). Unfortunately it probably just happened that the food source supported more dogs, so more dogs naturally stayed there.

Dogs live for the moment, for themselves, but they also live in social groups with us and that can sometimes lead to conflicts of interest between our wants, needs and desires, and theirs.

We have a choice. We can defer to our dogs and allow them to dictate to us in a variety of circumstances, but if we do that they will get an unrealistic perception of their status and expect to win in lots of other circumstances as well. Alternatively, we can make sure that they defer to us in as many situations as we can, so that we have the natural advantage in subsequent competitions.

In that case, how do we control their behaviour so that it doesn't conflict too much with our expectations, but without any confrontation, "alpha rolls", headlocks, half-nelsons, "three falls, two submissions or a knock-out" or other nonsense?

Casper is a Weimaraner who was having relationship trouble with his owner, Rob. Casper pulled on the lead, wouldn't come when called, refused to get in the car and growled when he was touched. If truth be told, he refused to do anything he was asked. It wasn't that he was unfriendly, a point he proved by jumping up at every person he met and putting his paws on their shoulders to lick their face.

The final straw came one balmy summer evening when Rob tied Casper's lead to the leg of the table in The Horse and Hound's beer garden. The pub cat wandered past and laughed at Casper, which was a serious mistake. Casper went for the cat and the cat went for the open kitchen door. Casper followed, dragging the table across the garden and only stopping when it jammed in the door frame. The chef was not amused to find Casper baying at the cat, which was perched on his pan rack, hissing. Rob had been dumped on the floor, soaked in beer. The glasses were smashed, the table was almost matchwood and Casper was banned from the pub for life. The other part of Casper's ASBO was an introduction to some rules.

Firstly, understand that dogs *like* rules. Every society needs rules to function. In our case they range from biblical commandments (for example, no killing people or coveting their asses) to household conventions (you don't get down from the table until you've eaten your parsnip). Without commonly accepted rules, societies fall apart.

If you don't know the rules in your society you can get into a lot of trouble because you don't know when you are breaking them ("Argh! He got down from the table without eating the parsnip! Stone him!").

We expect dogs to conform to our rules, like "don't pull on the lead", "don't dig up the roses", and "don't put your nose there", but they often don't seem to regard them with much importance. Lots of dogs fail to inhibit their behaviour and act in ways we consider to be inappropriate. Television abounds with programmes showing dogs misbehaving: biting, humping, fighting, jumping up and bouncing off the furniture. Many of them just don't know what is and isn't acceptable because of our inconsistency.

We often confuse our dogs with inconsistent rules like, "You can jump up on Uncle Peter", because he's big, strong and macho, and quite likes it, "but not on Aunty Wendy" because she is flattened to the floor and doesn't like it at all. Or "You can climb on my knee when you're dry, but not when you're wet", or, "You can eat the toast if it lands butter side down, but I want it back if it lands butter side up".

Far and away too complicated, confusing and unnecessary. No wonder most dogs don't know what the rules are.

If you don't know what the rules are, you've only got two choices. I'll give you an example. In the course of my work, I drive through speed-limited areas of 30mph, 40mph, 60mph and 70mph. There are several portable speed cameras that operate in the vicinity, but I can avoid being fined because I know what the rules are; where I must travel at 30, or where I can speed up to 40, 60 or 70.

If the rules were inconsistent, that is if they changed the speed limits around without telling me, I could either:

1. Not get into any trouble by travelling below the lowest speed limit all the way to work. Very frustrating. Very slow. Very depressing.

2. Not care about the cameras and drive how I like. I stand a good chance of picking up a punishment anyway, so what the heck. I can drive at 70 all the way. Fast, exciting. In fact, why stop at 70, I might as well be hung for a sheep as a lamb and do 80 – 90 – 100!

Dogs that don't know the rules can be depressed or live life in the fast lane. Mostly they opt for fast. They take a lot of punishment, but they get used to it. They throw themselves at the world and disregard everyone else. How difficult do you think it would be to train a dog as confused as that to come when called?

So, the first thing we must do for our dogs is to have a fixed set of rules, ones that are easy to understand, for example:

"You can jump up on people *only if invited*".

"You can climb on my knee *only if invited*".

"You can eat food from the floor *only if invited*".

Notice the common theme? Yes, there is only one rule: "You can do anything so long as it is OK with me".

To implement this rule we must have control of our dogs, not through confrontation, aggravation or aggression, but through them deferring to us. Our dog should *ask* if she can jump, climb or eat. It's only manners after all. You wouldn't expect me to jump on your knee without asking, would you? Why wouldn't I? Because in matters that concern your knee, I defer to you.

In that case, we need to instil a little deference in our dogs. A little consideration. A little respect. A little courtesy. How? By promoting ourselves. In any society, people or dogs who control the important things, control the little things by default. If you own the company, you own the paper clips as well.

So we need to control the important things, but the big question is: what's important to dogs? They don't care about things we think are important: the credit crunch, negative equity, shopping, globalisation, the hole in the ozone layer, or the fiscal performance of the longest serving labour government on record... So let's see what they do care about.

Chapter Seven

Good Manners

The Secrets of Control

Confusingly for both us and them, the three things dogs think are the most important in the world, we give away regularly, without a single thought. We not only give them to our dogs for free, we actually relinquish control of them.

Dogs frequently see themselves given control of the most important things in the world. How important must that make them feel? Like turning up for your first day as an office junior to be told, "Right-oh, yours is the plushest office with the biggest desk. You have staff to do your every bidding and a salary bigger than the company directors'. Would you like a cup of tea now? Chocolate biscuit?"

How difficult do you think it must be to train a dog as important as that to not to pull on a lead?

The start point for training a dog to do anything is to get the relationship right. Control the relationship and you control the dog.

What, then, are these magical resources that dogs find so important?

Food, games and us.

Control access to food, games and us and we control the dog. It's that easy? Well, maybe not that easy, but it's that simple. If we control the important things, dogs automatically assume we must control the incidental things as well. Things like the direction of the walk, when to go home, whether they can eat the road-kill they just found, when to stop barking at the doorbell, when to climb on our knee. Because we own the company, they don't take liberties with the paperclips.

Controlling food is the simplest, so we'll start with that. Remember that all food belongs to us. We went out and bought it with our hard earned cash and our dogs eat when we allow them to. I must emphasise that this is not the way to deal with dogs that already have a food-guarding problem. If your dog growls when you go near its food bowl, seek professional advice, you need it.

All we need to control food is to ask our dogs to say, "Please" each time we offer them any. No, I haven't gone bonkers, I know dogs can't speak and can't actually say, "Please", but they should ask our permission to eat. Look, I'll demonstrate with Sandy.

I take Sandy's food bowl, containing her dinner, and stand in front of her in the place I usually feed her. As I lower the food to the floor she dives towards it, so I calmly stand up with the bowl still in my hand and say, "Ah", the negative punishment signal that she is not going to get a reward for that behaviour. As her four legs hit the floor I again lower the bowl. She dives towards it and again I stand up and say, "Ah". This may happen a few times, but soon she will *not* dive at the bowl, as it's getting her nowhere. Immediately she *doesn't* dive in when I place the bowl on the floor (not letting go as I may need to pick it up quickly) I say, "Okay", the signal that she has done the right thing, and allow her to eat.

I am operantly conditioning the behaviour of "not diving in" by reinforcing it with the dinner. I have done it calmly, without confrontation, because I have a (slightly) larger brain and an opposable thumb.

She has quickly learned that "not diving in" gets her food. She deferred to me. Because I want her to say, "Please", next I'm going to ask for a particular behaviour from her. I'm going to ask her to sit. I don't even need to use the word "sit", but just wait until she sits and reinforce it with access to the food bowl. She will very quickly learn that sitting asks me to put her food down. Last week in puppy class, we taught a four-month-old Labrador to do this whilst in a class of nine other puppies. It took about thirty seconds. But Labradors are greedy aren't they? This one certainly was, that's what made him so quick to learn and easy to teach. If you really want the food, you learn fast.

Very quickly, we will have a dog that sits *at* us at mealtimes. Unfortunately, although it is a sign of the power of operant conditioning, it is also impolite. Our dog is saying, "Gimme my dinner!" which is not good enough. If she says, "Gimme" by sitting *at* me, I'm going to ask her to do something else, maybe a "down", or raise a paw. That way, she has always done something for me before I do something for her.

To control the food, that's all we have to do every time we want to give her anything, whether it is her main meal of the day or the corner from my toast, she has to do something for me, to say "please", before she gets it.

If we have to wait for mealtimes, we might only get one teaching opportunity a day, so there's a quick way of teaching food control that can also help us with other training. It integrates nicely with the obedience training we taught her in the last chapter.

We will need one dog, high value treats and some peace and quiet. It is dog training, so the previous knowledge of how dogs learn applies: don't start by trying to compete with distractions.

Sitting at dog level, facing our dog, we place a small treat on the palm of our hand, in front of her nose. The only words we are going to use are "Okay", "Ah" and feedback "Good girl" types. Again, do not try this if your dog suffers from food related aggression; you need specialist help.

When our dog tries to steal the treat from our hand, we close our fingers around it and say, "Ah". If we pull our hand away quickly she may well be tempted by the movement and try to follow it. This is not what we want, so we just wrap our fingers around the treat. We need to keep the hand in front of the dog and when she backs off trying to grab the treat, we can open it wide again. Most dogs try to grab again and we have to close the hand and say, "Ah" again. Grabbing does not get!

After a few, "Ah"s she will realise that she is not winning and back off even whilst the hand is open and the treat on display. At that point we can quickly say, "Okay" and give her the treat. We have reinforced the behaviour of "backing off the treat", with the treat. First Stage completed. Very neat!

Now we need to get Stage Two cracked. This is going to take a while, probably more than this session, and consists of repeating the process of "Ah" when she tries to grab and "Okay" when she backs off.

Eventually she will become so fluent that when we sit in front of her and open a hand with a treat in it, she will sit back and wait for us to say, "Okay" and give her the treat. She might sit for five, or even ten seconds. At this stage, we ask for more. The next time she backs off and doesn't take the treat, we're *not* going to say, "Okay" and deliver. We're just going to wait and use "Good girl" feedback.

She will shift about a bit, look at the floor, then back at the treat, then shift a bit more and, somewhere along the line, she will look us straight in the eye as if to say, "What do you want me to do then?" At that point we say, "Okay", and give her the treat. We just reinforced eye contact.

Occasionally a dog just does not make eye contact, often because there are previous negative associations

153

with it, and then we need to prompt her to look at us. I find a little squeaky noise, made by sucking my teeth, usually interests them enough to look at me. Saying your dog's name might work as well for you. Anything that works is fine.

Now, we're cookin'! We have a training process, still in its infancy, for asking our dog to look at us for instructions.

We withhold the treat again until we get eye contact, then prolong the eye contact for as long as it takes to say, "Good girl, Okay" and treat. The next time we prolong it with, "Good girl. Very clever. Okay" and treat.

The next time she is likely to look away, so we can tell her that looking away is not required with, "Ah", and as soon as she makes eye contact again, "Okay" and treat. Good timing is essential, and we are blessing my little cotton socks for practising with the "sit" in Chapter Four.

And coincidentally, we progress "eye contact" in the same way we progressed the "sit". Prolong the time she will look at us, but don't go on forever or she will look like a zombie. Reduce the feedback, start to introduce distractions and eventually phase out the treats onto a partial reinforcement ratio (remember slot machine payouts?).

We now have a dog that will look at us for instruction when we say, "Ah", so that we can communicate, "Don't do that, do this instead."

At the same time we have told her that we have first dibs on food. She has to defer to us for an important resource. We're gaining some history; a previous record of winning in the context of food. Now we're starting to become important, because we are controlling her access to one of the most important things in her world.

There is another way that our dog can try to control the food in her bowl, by not eating it. Oh, yes, I never said they weren't clever. Dogs all over the country are tucking into pan-fried breast of organic free-range chicken, gently sautéed in butter until tender, finely chopped and adorned with its own reduced jus.

Dogs can learn that if they don't eat, we either make a fuss of them or we give them something to make it more appetising. They are rewarded for not eating with attention or better food. "Not eating" becomes a way of controlling the situation.

If Brutus doesn't eat his tinned meaty chunks in gravy, we worry about him. Perhaps he doesn't like it? Perhaps I am a poor father? Shall I get him something else? Here you go Brutus, have my steak. Oh, look, he's gobbled that up. I'll not give him meaty chunks again!

I've known some owners go to the extent of hand feeding their poor mite. Bingo! Food and attention in one go. Who's controlling who?

Dogs evolved to eat low-grade human waste, the stuff we throw out. If we make sure it is nutritionally sound and relatively palatable, with no artificial additives or preservatives, we've done our bit. If Brutus is hungry, he will eat what we put in his bowl.

How do we change? Put your dog's food on the floor and leave it for ten minutes. If she doesn't eat it, she wasn't hungry enough. Pick it up and save it until next mealtime (or throw it away if you prefer). Next mealtime she gets the same ten minutes. When she is hungry, she will eat. No dog ever starved themselves to death when offered food. She learns that she eats when you give her the opportunity, not when she decides. If you feel bad about it, you can always keep the pan-fried chicken to teach some eye contact.

Next up, "Games". Why are games important? Unfortunately, humans have a casual view of games, as in, "It's only a game", and "It's child's play", so we tend not to rate them as terribly important. For most of our non-working pet dogs today, games are vital as the only way they can express their inherited predatory behaviour.

Games consist of using parts of the canine predatory sequences, although not necessarily in context, as anybody who has seen fly-ball games or any dog catching a Frisbee will realise.

In Chapter Three we looked at breed specific behaviour and why dogs need to exhibit it. Condensing that whole chapter into, "They like it" seems a bit superficial, but saves me repeating it all again here. In short, their brains are set up to find exhibiting predatory behaviour extremely rewarding.

If we don't allow our dogs to "work" in the function for which they were originally bred, they have a hole in their fulfilment. They are a Picasso with no canvass, a Pele with no ball, a Popeye with no spinach, a Presley with no stage. Often they will spontaneously break out into predatory behaviour in an effort to achieve that gratification: retrievers "steal" socks; collies chase cars; staffies pounce on lights and shadows. This is a measure of the value of the brain chemistry reward. Using up that energy on toys and games is far more appropriate and keeps them out of trouble.

If it is that rewarding (and it is), how important does it make us if we have control of the outlet for it? Right up there with God and Obi-Wan Kenobi, depending upon your religion. You become her own superhero, but without having to wear your underpants on the outside.

The first thing we must do is take control of her toys. There are two kinds of toys: the ones she plays with on her own and the ones we use to play with her.

Pick up all of our dog's toys and place them in a toy box. We probably don't need an ornate wooden chest with the word "TOYS" stencilled on the lid; a carrier bag on the back of the kitchen door will do, but make it somewhere she can't get at. Now we own the toys, we can give her some back again to play with. It is fine for her to keep *these* toys in her own "toy box" to which she has constant access. Each day we can give her two or three toys from the toy box for her to play with and pick up the previous day's.

This has two major effects. The first is that she will play with her toys more. Constant access to anything devalues it. If you went to the pictures every night it would soon become a chore rather than a treat; chocolate for every meal sounds good to start with, but the novelty soon wears off. Likewise, can you remember when your dog found an old toy or bone, long lost in the shrubbery, and it suddenly becomes her most treasured possession? Restricting access to anything increases its value.

"If the squeaky carrot isn't there all the time, I'd better play with it whilst I have the chance." Tomorrow the squeaky carrot is gone, but the rubber chicken is there. Different toys every day is nearly as good as new toys every day.

The second major effect is that it increases *our* value. Now toys are available only through us, we become "THE KEEPER OF THE TOYS", with our "carrier bag of power".

Next thing to do is a little more difficult, but the theory is the same. We control the games, too. When we play with our dogs, whatever we play with our dogs should be under our control. We decide when to start, continue and stop. There are several considerations here.

Firstly, *what* we play. If we can't control the game, we shouldn't be playing it. Remember it is the dog's perception of control that is important, because the ultimate aim is to persuade her that we control all the important things in her life. I don't mind anyone playing rough and tumble rolling about, or any other test of strength, such as "play fighting", or tug of war, so long as the dog thinks you win.

Allowing her to win gives her the impression that she can beat us some of the time. It lacks consistency and encourages confrontation. "It's only a game"? Not to our dog it isn't, it's a competition. Just think, if she can nearly beat me, she must think a six-year-old girl will be easy.

Some books recommend that you *never* play tug of war with your dog for exactly the same reasons, and it is easy to see how the mistake can be made. However, I think that we *can* win tug of war every time, by the ingenious device of having two tug toys and opposable thumbs. When we want her to let go of the first, so that we win, we wave the second. When we want to finish, we wave the other tug and keep both. Or swap it for a food treat. We always win the overall competition.

Other good games? Chasing, retrieving and searching. What we play *with* should always belong to us. We bring it out when we want to play and keep it when we finish. It is our special play toy, not one of the ones from the toy box, because this is a higher quality game and it is only available through us.

Which brings us on to *when* we play. Our dog might demand play from time to time. This is not polite behaviour, because she hasn't said "please". In the same way that we ask for a deferential behaviour before we feed her, we can also take control of when we play by asking for one then, too. Alternatively, if she is very demanding, bouncy and pushy, we can say, "Sorry, bit busy right at the moment." and ignore her until she settles down, when we

160

can say, "Right-oh, let's play now." thus rewarding quieter behaviour with the opportunity to play.

The toughest bit to judge is when she is getting fed-up and about to stop playing. We should stop just a tiny bit ahead of her, so *we* finish the game, not her. Controlling the end of a game and putting the toy back in our pocket is just as important as starting it.

Not only should we control the games, we should also control the access to the games. Casper the friendly Weimaraner used to leap about and run round the room every time his lead was produced. Rob had to grapple him to the floor to clip it on. Then there was a fight at the door, as Casper tried to barge through it before it was opened. He looked forward to the wrestling match as a great game, but Rob didn't.

We calmed him down by stopping trying to physically control Casper and starting to control the situation. Having previously taught Casper eye contact and a 'sit' on command, whenever Rob produced his lead he asked him to sit. If he didn't, the lead was put away again and Rob sat down to read the paper. Very quickly, Casper got the idea that if he didn't sit, the lead went away. When he sat, Rob clipped the lead on without fuss.

Next, to the door. With Casper on the lead at the door, Rob asked him to sit again. Casper not only sat, but made eye contact as well. However, when Rob placed his hand on the door handle, he lunged at the door. Rob took his hand away and said, "Ah", to signal that the behaviour would not be rewarded, and Casper made eye contact again. Over the next few minutes, Casper learned that if he got up from the sit, the door closed, but if he sat and made eye contact it opened progressively wider, until Rob was able to fully open the door with Casper still sitting and looking at him. At that point Rob was able to say, "Off you go then", and allow Casper through.

As you can see, control is not about who goes through the door first (another "dominance" myth), but who controls the door. Our clever use of door handles allows us an edge over our dogs and so we can decide when they go out. They must defer to us to gain access to this very important resource.

We now control food and games. The last one is the toughie: Us. Or, more specifically, our attention. Dogs are attention sponges, they soak it up and come looking for more. By some quirk of nature we have managed to breed animals that can consume more than their own weight in attention every second (this is not a scientific measurement).

We'd better define what attention is, and its value to dogs. Attention, in this sense, is any form of communication with our dog. A touch, a word, a fleeting look; whether heartfelt oratory or a passing glance. Why is it valuable? It's valuable because so many good things come from us, because they are attached to us, and because the opposite, being ignored and alone, makes any social animal feel bad. Even punishing attention can be better than none at all. We all crave attention from our fellows. Why was being sent to bed a punishment? No social animal likes exclusion, and dogs are no exception.

"Attached to us" has a special scientific meaning in this context, and we'll look at that later from the perspective of puppy development, but for now it roughly means that they have bonded with us emotionally and they use us to cope with life's difficult patches. If they were humans we would be allowed to say that they "love" us but that would be terribly anthropomorphic.

You can get very strict programmes for dealing with problem dogs that constantly seek attention in particularly inappropriate ways, but we needn't go into that depth. We need some guidance that allows us to control what we do with our attention. After all, there can be little argument that we really do actually own ourselves!

Again, the concept is simple, but putting it into practice can be more difficult. For example, if I said, "ignore your dog when it actively seeks attention", that is very good advice, but how many people can prevent themselves from stroking the Labrador head that appears ever so gently out of nowhere onto your knee when you're reading the paper? Not me! My first explosives search Labrador, Dan, had it off to a fine art. He would wait until I was distracted, about five minutes into reading, then his head would s-l-o-w-l-y creep onto my knee and before I knew it, I was fondling behind his ears!

Would I want to stop that kind of attention seeking? Not really, that's what we have dogs for; the part of the "attachment" that goes both ways.

So, what part of our attention do we want to place under our control? The part that is gained in ways we don't like. This isn't about depriving our dogs of attention, far from it, it is about making sure that they say "please" rather than "gimme", and allowing us to occasionally say "not now".

The process, too, is simple. When our dog performs behaviours like biting fingers or barking at us, she is saying, "Look at me! Look at me!" She wants our attention.

The reasons can be many, from boredom, lack of exercise or unfulfilled breed specific behaviour, to learned stress. She is trying to maximise her chances of a reaction from us. Now, bear in mind that any attention is better than no attention at all (that's why coming downstairs at 3am and yelling at a howling puppy is counterproductive), so shouting "No!", smacking and chasing are actually going to reward the behaviour. "Yippee! Let's play the game where I bite your fingers then try to avoid being hit!"

Examined closely, our dog is performing a behaviour to produce a reward for herself (self learned operant conditioning), but she is controlling the situation.

What we need to do is to place attention-demanding behaviours under our control. How? By ignoring them, not passively, but actively. Any behaviour our dog performs that is designed to get a reaction out of us needs to be thwarted by the withdrawal of our attention. This shows her that the inappropriate behaviour actually has an adverse result, rather than a reward. Ignoring her by removing our attention is a big signal, too. "You do that behaviour and I leave", is hard to misunderstand. Remember the definitions? It is negative punishment: we take away something she likes, our attention, and that makes her avoid repeating the behaviour.

A word on ignoring: "passive ignoring" is just getting on with whatever we are doing despite the dog tugging on our trouser leg. It is difficult to make it work, as she will just try harder and harder until it is impossible to take no notice. Then she gets a reaction which proves that if she tries hard enough trouser tugging *will* work.

"Active ignoring" comes in a scale of intensities. At the top end of the scale, as soon as she looks at the trouser leg we walk out of the door and close it behind us. Next down, useful for behaviours like jumping, is to stand up, turn our back, fold our arms, don't speak and look at the ceiling (to remove the possibility of eye contact). If she knows a word for the absence of reward (for example "Ah"), we can use that, just once, as we leave or turn.

In the initial stages of changing a relationship, we need to use these intensities to ensure that she doesn't persist with the behaviour. We want a big (negative) punishment for bad behaviour, so total removal of attention is best. Later on, when she understands that "turning" signals our intention to remove our attention, we can reduce the signal to the merest turn of the head.

We wait until she stops the behaviour and then count to three. Any longer than that and she has forgotten what she was punished for. Quite often, when we turn around, she will be sitting, looking perplexed. When we go back into the room, or turn around, and this is the most important bit, give her something else to do that we can reward for all we are worth.

The whole process looks like this:

Dog tugs at trouser leg to get attention.

We walk out of the room and close the door, then count to three.

We go back in when she is sitting looking perplexed.

We say, "Go fetch your rubber chicken".

When she does, we play a game.

This punishes the behaviour of *leg tugging*, but rewards the behaviour of *rubber chicken fetching*. After a time she learns that *chicken fetching* results in a game and *leg tugging* results in social exclusion.

We replace the bad behaviour by rewarding an alternative with the very thing she wanted in the first place. But now it is under our control. The behaviour bods call it Differential Reinforcement of Incompatible behaviour (or DRI), but for me it is a beautifully circular way of taking control of our attention. It teaches the dog precisely what we find acceptable by reinforcing the behaviour we like with exactly what she wanted in the first place, and it will work for anything.

Often, less able dog trainers only provide attention when the dog is misbehaving, in the form of "Stop that, lie down! Argh! Get off!" and tend to ignore dogs that aren't causing them a problem. This is the complete opposite of what works. From the dog's point of view the only reward she gets is when she is misbehaving; there's no reinforcement in sitting quietly!

The people who make the best dog trainers are constantly assessing what they reinforce and what they ignore. Attention is a powerful tool and dogs will work very hard to obtain it. If we provide it when we like what she does and remove it when we don't like what she does, it not only remains ours to control, but it also means that she is working towards good behaviour all the time. Even better, if we can head our dog off at the pass, so to speak, and give her the preferable alternative *before* the she feels she need to perform the inappropriate behaviour, we can avoid all punishment and direct our dog towards a more rewarding lifestyle. So, if we can predict when the trouser-tugging is *about* to take place, and ask her to bring a toy *before* she does it, she'll stop doing it in favour of toy-fetching.

Well, we did it. Rob took control of the most important things in Casper's life: food, games and attention. Now

Casper says "please" when he wants anything important, he knows food belongs to Rob so he looks to him for permission before eating anything, he plays games where Rob wins, by invitation only, and he knows that performing good behaviour gets him some good quality attention. We needed some specific training to stop him jumping at people and to get him into the car, but the crux of the whole problem was the mismatch in Casper and Rob's relationship. Get your connection with your dog right and everything else flows from it.

The last two chapters have been all about our relationship with our dogs and how to control them so that we live together in peace and harmony, but why bother? Well, not only does it make life more pleasant for both of us, it also makes training our dogs to do anything much easier. Our dog listens to us; she defers to us to earn all the rewards she finds valuable. How easy do you think it is going to be to train a dog like that to come when called?

We've been looking at our relationship with an individual dog and in that relationship we have been making allowances for individual preferences. Some dogs prefer cheese to hotdogs, some prefer pointing to chasing, and we've partially explained those preferences by examining breed specific behaviour, but that's not the whole story. Not many years ago, as the study of genetics was leaving its infancy and gangling towards its spotty adolescence, there was a huge debate on whether breeding or upbringing had the biggest effect upon an individual. You might remember it as Nature versus Nurture?

Well, having looked at the nature of dogs, it is time to look at how nurture affects them.

Chapter Eight
Puppy Development

The Secret of How to Grow a Puppy

I am going to assume that we want our dog to develop into a normal family pet. Most of the principles we'll be using will apply to dogs brought up for other purposes, for example police or assistance work, but some purposes, such as guarding property or sheep, necessitate different priorities. What I want to aim for is what I hope most pet dog owners want: a well-balanced companion.

We already know that the Nature versus Nurture debate is a false one because neither can function without the other. If I don't have the genes that make growing long legs possible, it doesn't matter how much or little food I eat as I grow up, I won't have long legs. If a dog doesn't have the genes that make chasing behaviour possible, it doesn't matter how often a rabbit runs past, it can't develop chasing behaviour. Alternatively, a dog with the chase genes that never plays chase games won't develop its full chasing potential.

Genes and environment complement each other in the development of any and every individual. The genes operate on the environment and the environment operates on the genes. In a very real way, genes *are* the environment.

The first point at which we can have an influence is in the selection of our new pup's parents. We need to look for the genetic stock we want.

First cautionary note: All the studies of fearfulness in dogs show that like begets like, which means that if one of their parents is a scaredy-cat, pups will probably be as scared and maybe a bit more. Within half a dozen or so generations it is possible to breed pups that are frightened witless, even when starting with normal, lovely, friendly dogs. If mum doesn't come out to meet you, wagging her tail and smiling all over her face, don't buy the puppy.

Second cautionary tale:

Mr and Mrs Addison are an elderly, non-too-sprightly couple, who came to my training class with Fleabit, their ten-month-old working cocker spaniel bitch. "She runs off on walks and won't come back." they told me. Trying to work out how difficult the task ahead was, I enquired as to what, exactly, she did when she ran off. "She doesn't go far, she just sniffs the ground and runs about." "Not too bad", I thought, "What have you tried to get her back?"

"Everything, from whistles to an electric collar."

"Sorry, a "what"?" I looked down at the big brown eyes that were gazing up at me through three and a half kilos of fluff and ears.

"We went to a gundog trainer and he lent us a collar that gave her an electric shock when she didn't come back."

"Did it work?" I knew it was a stupid question, because they wouldn't be sitting in front of me if it had, but I was still in shock, myself. "It worked for a couple of times, but then she just used to kind of leap up in the air and run off again."

"Good grief! But tell me, why did you get a *working* cocker spaniel?"

"Well, we've always had show-bred cocker spaniels before and we thought the working type had shorter hair and would be easier to keep clean."

Show-bred cocker spaniels are specially selected from a long line of dogs that have learned to stand prettily and not bite a judge. Working ones come from a long line of manic searchers. Fleabit was prepared to carry on searching despite being electrocuted for doing it. If you want a dog with that kind of determination, you need to select it carefully.

"Like begets like" means that if you buy a working cocker spaniel pup she will grow up into the same behaviour her parents had. The clue is in the name. It is not a difficult concept; what you breed from is what you get.

Over the last ten years or so there has been a popular explosion in the understanding of a concept originally called "socialisation" and this was later extended to include a related process called "environmental conditioning" or "habituation". Almost every responsible puppy owner knows that it is necessary for the future wellbeing of their pup, but what exactly does it mean?

Socialisation is introducing puppy to a variety of people and animals, and environmental conditioning

174

introduces her to things in the environment, from vacuum cleaners to thunder. Together these prepare the puppy for her future life by allowing her to learn the behaviour patterns acceptable for the society and surroundings in which she is going to live. For reasons of brevity, I'm going to lump them together in the commonly accepted term "socialisation".

Why is it important? Well, in the natural environment an original dog would live alongside its little gang and not see much more than the edge of a village. These days we ask them to interact with a huge variety of weird looking dogs, all manner of other animals, vast crowds of even stranger looking people and a world full of wonderful things from fireworks to traffic. The Association of Pet Behaviour Counsellors' figures show that between a fifth and a quarter of all canine behaviour problems relate directly to a lack of early social and environmental experience and suggest that an even bigger proportion may be indirectly linked, for example through a subsequent lack of confidence or undue fearfulness.

As usual, whenever a concept becomes popular there are lots of misconceptions thrown into the mix, often by mystical dog trainers who know somebody who was once told about it, so we need to sort out the scientific wheat from the mythical chaff.

Let's start with what socialisation isn't. It definitely isn't taking your pup to one puppy socialisation class when it is fourteen weeks old. It starts way before that...

Accepting that puppy development starts with the genetic material that they inherit from their parents and that we can only work within those limits, the first time we can have any input is on the developing embryo. Yes, really. We can start to prepare our puppy for their future life before they are even born.

Studies into species as varied as blue foxes, humans, rats, rhesus monkeys, baboons and guinea pigs have all found that when a mother is severely stressed, the foetus inside her grows into an adult less able to cope with stress than others of their species. This should not be surprising; a foetus shares the same hormonal environment as their mother. If the mother is awash with stress hormones, the baby will be too.

In real terms that means if you over-stress a bitch when she is carrying pups, the pups will be a little less able to cope with the stresses of modern dog life. They are likely to be shy, not good with other dogs and strange people, and not confident when presented with something new.

Where do you think that leaves pups from puppy farms? Do we think puppy farms are likely to stress a bitch? The cop-out answer is, "depends on the puppy farm," but if I'm choosing a pup I want her mum to have been nurtured in the bosom of her family right throughout her pregnancy. No undue stress at all. A happy mum in a happy place. (Incidentally, mild to moderate stress, as happens to us all every day, actually helps the ability to cope – we need a bit of stress.)

So, we breed from sound temperaments and chose parents with behaviour we like. We pamper mum when she is expecting and in due course our pup meets the world.

It wasn't really until the late 1950s and early 60s that scientists started to pay attention to the behavioural development of dogs and what consequences different forms of upbringing had for the adult. Even then, most of the experiments took the form of isolating the pups in one way or another and seeing how they turned out.

This in turn grew out of studies of showing that goslings "imprinted" upon the first moving object they saw in the hours soon after hatching. They then followed that object as though it was their mum. Genetically, this makes excellent sense, as the object wild goslings most often see is a mother goose. Occasionally, when it is a bearded scientist, they follow him around instead. In the 1930's this was regarded as hilarious, but remember that not many people had television back then, and most of life was in black and white.

This period during which imprinting was possible was defined as "critical" because it only had a certain window of opportunity. If it was missed, imprinting became almost impossible. The effects have since been proved to be reversible, but not easily.

Studies into what was suspected to be a critical period for the socialisation of puppies started to blossom and it has probably turned into one of the most scrutinized areas of dogs' lives. We know more about the early physical and behavioural development of dogs than almost any other aspect of them. And it is a good job too, because it turns out it is immensely important.

To understand "socialisation", we need to understand the importance of a term of which most people won't have heard: the "species template". No animal is born knowing the species to which they belong. All animals have a period during which they are most susceptible to learning their species identity from the animals around them.

To have a wide species template is to be like the ducks, geese and chickens that can imprint upon almost anything, from hairy scientists to cardboard cut-outs and red balloons (I kid you not, that was another experiment).

To have a narrow species template is to restrict the criteria that an animal will accept when seeking an identity. The modern wolf has a narrow species identity template that can only be widened if the dam is not present during the sensitive period. If the dam is there the pups will only socialise to her and will exclude any other species. This is one of the reasons they are difficult to tame. The existence of a wide template is not common in animals generally, but *is* common in domesticated animals and may be an important prerequisite in the domestication of larger species.

Dogs have a wide template that will accommodate multiple species and, as usual, scientists have pushed the boundaries by socialising puppies not only with the obvious choice, cats, but also with rabbits and sheep, and of course we do it every day with people.

Practically, this means that dogs will regard lots of species as being socially relevant. They don't actually think they are cats, rabbits or people, but they regard them as being worthy of displaying social behaviour towards. They interact with them as though they can understand dog behaviour. They "talk" to them as though they are dogs.

The period during which this process can happen is defined as a "critical period" in geese and the like, because it lasts only for about the first 36 hours after hatching and is then lost. In dogs it is now called a "sensitive period" because it lasts considerably longer and is less well defined at the edges. It is not a few "critical" days, but rather a period during which puppies are sensitive to the possibilities of socialisation.

However we need to rewind a bit, because the sensitive period for socialisation does not take place straight after birth, like it does in fowl. Puppies are born blind and deaf, how can they learn what species they belong to if they can't see or hear?

The pressure of genetic selection has honed the development of puppy behaviour to the finest point. Called "ontogeny" it means that the genes responsible for each phase of development turn the right behaviour on at exactly the right time. For example, the ability to suck is turned on two days before they are born and turns off at ten to fourteen weeks (honest, adult dogs can't suckle properly). Any sooner or later would be wasteful because they don't need it. We'll come back to ontogeny later.

The exact timing of the onset and offset of the period for socialising our pup and the amount of interaction necessary have been the subject of much scientific debate and, as you'd expect, lots of studies. One found that you could socialise pups to humans with only two twenty minute periods of interaction per week, but their definition of "socialise" was a bit different to what we want; it meant the pup wasn't too scared of people to approach them (and there were no follow-up studies of how they turned out as adults). It was originally thought the sensitive period started about three weeks and ended about ten to fourteen weeks of age, but everybody really knew that the boundaries were more blurred than that, so looked for a better theory. After all, that's what science is about, looking for better theories.

The next best theory to come along proposed that the socialisation period ended with the onset of a "fear response" and although this was still usually at about ten to fourteen weeks, at least it gave us a positive marker for individuals. What's a "fear response"? It is when a puppy first barks like she is scared: front end up, back end down, ears down and back, lips like a funnel, tail between the legs, and aimed at something she now doesn't like; or when she starts to hide from scary things. The fear response was thought to be ontogenetic; that is, it just switched on at a predetermined time, in the same way the milk teeth are replaced at a given time.

Some still hold to this theory, but it remains a bit vague. The problem is that you can't predict when the fear response will start and it can be very variable from breed to breed, even pedigree lines within a breed and right down to individuals within a litter. All agree, however that you need to get the bulk of your socialising done before the fear response stops you, because socialising is about being introduced to new experiences. If you are afraid of new experiences, then it follows that you can't socialise to them after you have developed a fear response.

Again, everybody lived with the theory but knew it didn't explain everything, because we all had experience of socialising dogs *after* they started displaying a fear response. A puppy doesn't bark at *every* new thing she sees after fourteen weeks old, does she?

The theory I like best proposes that the sensitive period for socialisation is actually better named a period of "behavioural organisation" and that, at the age of three weeks, puppies start a mental process that builds a set of experiences that prepare them for their whole life.

To understand why we have to delve a little into neurophysiology. Don't worry, with a little simplification, it won't hurt.

Adult mammals have two competing physiological nervous systems over which we have no control. One is the "sympathetic autonomic nervous system" and the other is the "parasympathetic autonomic nervous system" and they are there to regulate our body state. You may have heard of "fight or flight"? That is the "sympathetic autonomic response". Amongst its effects are: our heart rate increases, pupils dilate, lungs open, we sweat, our hair stands on end and blood glucose levels rise to provide energy to our muscles. These all prepare us for action in response to some kind of threat. We are in a state of mental and physical arousal.

The parasympathetic autonomic response has the opposite effect. It brings us down, relaxes our body and we are no longer tense. We are not stressed.

Obviously, the "sympathetic" prepares us for "fight or flight" when confronted by something of which we are afraid. The "parasympathetic" brings back down to normal again afterwards.

Before they are three weeks of age, there is comparatively little brain activity in a puppy. The pup's brain, like other organs, has not developed sufficiently, so it can't take in a great deal. After that, as eyes and ears open and the brain connections start to be made, information can be stored and used.

Now comes the important bit. Before about five weeks old, the parasympathetic autonomic is the dominant system in puppies' brains. No, that is important, read it again. They find it really difficult to get stressed or anxious. No "fight or flight". They can't have a fear response

183

because the brain can't support one. They are relaxed. Within reason, it doesn't matter what they see or hear, they won't be afraid.

During this period puppies build up a "maintenance set" of experiences. What this means is that the things they are subjected to during the period of parasympathetic dominance are recorded in the brain as being normal. The pup collects a series of experiences it considers to be non-threatening. Afterwards, anything that they come into contact with is compared to the information in the maintenance set to see if it can be categorised as normal, or not. Depending upon how near to normal the new experience is, it can be labelled "okay" and added to the maintenance set, or as "not normal", which equals "scary" and to be avoided.

By this process the brain builds a picture of what is normal in the puppy's environment. Between about five and eight weeks there is a period of sympathetic dominance, as the puppy's brain continues to develop. During this time the pup has the capacity to be seriously worried about new things that don't fit the maintenance set. It therefore follows that the more experiences that go into the maintenance set between three and five weeks, the more likely it is that a new one will be similar enough to one of them to be labelled "normal" too.

One study showed that puppies exposed to video images of household items like vacuum cleaners and toy balls between three and five weeks old, were later found to be less fearful of the actual items than puppies that had not seen the pictures on screen.

The pups, having seen pictures of a vacuum cleaner, placed them in a maintenance set. When they saw the actual cleaner it was close enough to the picture for them to understand it was no threat.

Experienced pup: Question. "What is this upright moving thing with a bag and a humming noise?"

Answer. "I don't know, but it is like that thing I saw two weeks ago and that didn't hurt me".

Inexperienced pup: Question. "What is this upright moving thing with a bag and a humming noise?"

Answer. "I don't know. It's like nothing I've ever seen before. Help!"

It is easy to see how the process is self-perpetuating. With enough experience to build up a large set of things that are not scary, when the period of parasympathetic dominance ends, at about five weeks, the pup will still not be afraid of new things because most new things are like things it has already experienced! Continued experience continues to build more into the maintenance set.

Let's use the vacuum cleaner as an example. Vacuum cleaners are things on wheels that move, make a humming noise and blow air. We puppies are not afraid of vacuum cleaners because we are familiar with them. This gives us experience of things moving on wheels, humming things and things that blow air. Now, for the first time, we experience hair dryers. They make the humming noise and blow air, which is close enough to vacuum cleaners for us to place them in the "okay" category.

Toy cars make a noise, and move on wheels; they're okay, then.

Electric drills? Noise, airflow but no wheeled movement: okay.

Lawn mowers? Noise, air blowing and wheel movement: okay.

Bicycles? Less noise but more movement on wheels: okay.

Prams? Less of everything: okay.

Motorbikes? They're just a cross between a bicycle and a lawn mower: okay.

Cars? Okay. Buses? Okay. Huge juggernauts? Okay. Trains? Okay. Low flying military aircraft? Okay.

You see how the set of things that are "okay" builds *on itself* from a modest start? And that's only from vacuum cleaners. Maybe a bit oversimplified, but you get the picture.

We're going to return to "maintenance sets" later, but for now, back to socialising our puppy.

As I said, puppies are born blind and deaf. For the next two to three weeks, known as the neonatal period (neo = new and natal = born) they do little but sleep and suckle from mum, but even during this time of apparent inability to react, we can affect their future behaviour. How?

Easy; a couple of times a day we can gently pick them up, cuddle them, stroke them and talk quietly to them. The experience will be new, but comfortable and safe.

We are getting the pups used to the smell, feel, sound and sight of humans. Although born with restricted senses, they don't all suddenly switch on at once. They start to hear a little more each day as their ears develop. I was too young to be able to remember when it happened to me, but I bet the first sounds are muffled and distant, becoming louder and clearer with time. If we expose the pups to the "people experience" a little each day, by the time their senses are fully functional we will be as normal as their littermates!

There's something else we can do, that follows on from this, too. I mentioned earlier that I would want my future pup to be born to a bitch nurtured in the bosom of her family. I want that family to be a noisy boisterous one. I want a pup that's been born in the kitchen, with the radio on, kids playing, washing machine tumbling and kettle screeching. So long as that is normal for the mum, the pups will grow up thinking it normal, too.

Bonzo was a Boxer with aggression. "He's okay with us and the kids," said Alan, "so long as we don't make any loud noises". Alan got Bonzo from a friend as a present for his partner. He was the last pup to go from a litter of six.

His friend lived alone and was trying to sell his house, so didn't want the pups cluttering up the place when prospective buyers came round. He had emptied the garage and put his bitch's whelping box in the corner. The garage was quite large and gave them room to run about without going outside. He advertised the pups when they were six weeks old, but they didn't sell well. At eight weeks he took the bitch away, back into the house, because she seemed fed up of the pups and growled at them all the time. Eventually, as the price came down, the pups sold one by one, until, at sixteen weeks old, only Bonzo was left. At eighteen weeks, still in the garage, Bonzo at last found his new home.

Everything seemed to be fine, for a while. Bonzo mostly stayed under the chair in the kitchen, so they fed him there. When he got used to family life he would come out to play but if the kids yelled too loudly he always scooted back under the chair.

He never really enjoyed going out and always avoided new people and especially dogs, if he could. But now Bonzo was fourteen months old, and had wrecked the vet's surgery when he went for his booster jab. They knew he didn't want to be there, but they hadn't counted on the level of aggression he was prepared to use to get out. Both Alan and Josie, his partner, had been bitten as they grappled with him. Several other dogs had been traumatised in the ten minutes he had been in the waiting room and the vet suggested Bonzo might have a serious problem.

Can you imagine being a pup born in an empty garage? You might be warm and comfortable cuddled up to mum, but you are never subjected to normal family life. As your senses develop, there is no input. It is dark-ish, quiet and you only see a human once a day when a bloke turns up to feed your mum. You have no experience outside mum and littermates. Everything that we think of as being normal: radios, stairs, cats, children, vacuum cleaners, doorbells, kettles, the list is endless, would be outside what you could cope with. How stressing do you think that might be when you first meet a couple of children? How frightened do you think that pup is going to be when, at eight weeks old, she is sold into a normal family? I'll tell you. She will be terrified, and it will probably harm her for life.

If you have a quiet house for your pups, there are recordings on the market that simulate a normal family, but a CD is no match for the real thing.

Pups are gifted with a period of parasympathetic dominance between about three and five weeks (may be sooner or later by a few days), when they are able to start building a group of experiences that they consider normal. After that, provided they can relate a new experience to one already in the memory bank, they won't be afraid of it. Each time a new benign event happens, they can add that in too. Obviously, the more they experience without being worried, the more they *can* experience without being worried! And it doesn't stop, like we used to suppose; it carries on for good. Not just for pups, but right up into adulthood and beyond.

This is where the theory differs from the usual concept of socialisation. There is no "critical" period, and the "sensitive" period is only sensitive because such a young puppy has nothing with which to compare incoming information.

All dogs carry round their own maintenance set of experiences with which they judge each new event they come across; if it is the same or similar to a previous non-threatening one, they aren't worried. They continue to make these judgements throughout their life.

What can we owners do? We can make sure that new experiences actually are non-threatening until they have built up a decent sized maintenance set of their own.

So, how are we going to do that? Well, some things are innately frightening, like being startled by a loud noise, and this is where the CDs can come in handy. If we play the sound of fireworks quietly, when bonfire night comes around our pup will not be as worried because she has heard them before.

When she meets strange dogs, we can make sure that the outcome is pleasant rather than scary. In fact, we can expose her to all kinds of environmental and social situations provided we know they are going to turn out well.

The negative side of this is that if there is little or no information collected between three and five weeks, almost everything she meets after that will be scary. Bear in mind that although we aim to build a set of things that have nice outcomes, we also have the capacity to build a set of situations that have nasty outcomes. Be attacked by a black Labrador dog and you start to worry about all black dogs. Have your ears pulled by one small child and you start to worry about all small children.

When do we stop? Never. Puppy socialisation never stops; neither does adult dog socialisation (although I think we might have to adopt the term "behavioural organisation"). Forget about fourteen weeks and forget about the fear response. If she exhibits a fear response, we got it wrong by not ensuring the experience was nice enough for her maintenance set. Through our mistake we have probably included it in the set of "things to avoid". Experience builds upon experience upon experience. The more good experiences she has the more she expects the next one to be good. Likewise the more bad experiences she has the more she worries about the next one.

This theory allows for what all good dog trainers know: that even if a pup has had a restricted early environment, it is still possible, with great care and a lot of patience, to get them to the stage where they can cope with everyday life. It is not as good as an enriched early environment, but is still possible, and that is what was missing in the depictions of sensitive periods that ended abruptly at fourteen weeks or at the onset of the fear response.

The next question is, "What type of experiences should go in the maintenance set?" The answer comes in two parts:

Firstly all dogs need to be able to communicate with their own species and we know that most face-to-face dog communication is through body language (nose-to-bum communication is by scent). Our puppy's dilemma is that the dogs out there in the world look nothing like her mum or brothers and sisters, so how can she use her experience with them? She can't, but, as usual, the evolution of puppy development has the answer. She gives off, "I'm a puppy, don't hurt me," signals, so she can get close to other dogs and then picks up on what they are saying back. She learns about all the different types of pricked, long, short and dropped ears, the fuzzy faces with long or short noses, and so on, covering as many types as she sees. One experiment showed that up to five different dogs in the same house was not enough variety for puppies to generalise their communication skills to other dogs. She needs to see a lot of dogs to fit communication skills in her maintenance set.

Have you seen the varieties people come in? Long, short, fat, thin, old and young, hairy or bald, in uniform, carrying brollies... need I go on? She also needs to see a wide variety of people, so she can include them in her set. Children are particularly difficult to understand; they run about unpredictably, wave their arms and yell, in ways that adults tend not to.

The second part of the answer is a bit more vague, I'm afraid, because it is specific to each puppy and is: "Whatever you want your dog to see when it grows up". If you live on a farm, it might be sheep; if you live in the town it might be buses. If you live in a circus it might be elephants; if you live where I do, it will be low flying military aircraft. The pup needs to be shown all the things in the environment in which it is to grow up.

So where do things like puppy classes fit in? Do you need a puppy class? Well, not if you've access to a wide variety of dogs and people with which to socialise your pup, but if you haven't, then puppy classes are good way to do it. Good puppy classes are a structured way for pups to collect new information about the world in an agreeable way. They should allow well-mannered exposure to other dogs, people and situations, with positive outcomes.

Puppy classes can be bad if they involve any threatening situations, like being bounced upon by a boxer, nipped by a collie or scared by an overbearing trainer.

There are a lot of poor puppy classes where dogs play with each other for an hour then go home. These pups learn either that they can beat up other dogs, or that other dogs beat them up. Neither of these is a good idea. Find a good puppy class.

We did a lot of work with Bonzo, and continue to do so, teaching him relaxation exercises and introducing him to a variety of everyday sights and sounds in a controlled way, and he is getting better. His stress has to be constantly monitored and his life managed so that he is able to cope. We never assume he is 'fixed', because there is always the chance that a combination of factors will tip him over the edge again, like it did in the vet's surgery, but eighteen months down the line he continues to improve.

So, that's "socialisation" for you, the process by which your dog learns who and what is scary, or not. Manage it carefully; it is the making of your puppy.

There are other important issues for your pup as she develops; not least her relationship with you and how she uses it. Although we discussed dog/human relationships in Chapter Five, I purposely left out one aspect that fits in better with puppy development: "attachment".

Attachment is the process by which dogs bond with people/dogs. When it happens between people we call it "love". Hence you love your kids, your mum and your significant other. We attach to people who are important to us, in varying degrees. We prefer some of them to others.

Dogs do this too and they have an easy mechanism for it. The only thing necessary for a dog to become attached to an individual (dog or person) is proximity. Any individual a pup spends time with will become an attachment figure.

The individual that a pup spends most *quality* time with becomes the primary attachment figure. This is the figure that we take our cues from. We try to emulate our primary attachment figure. We use our primary attachment figure as a coping mechanism. When we get into emotional trouble (frightened, worried, anxious) we refer to our primary attachment figure for guidance.

In dog terms, when they have a problem they look to the primary attachment figure for help. They can cope so long as they have that help. That primary attachment figure needs to be you.

This might be problematic if your pup lives with another dog. Eight to ten hours of quality play with another dog means that they might attach to the other dog more than to you. You would become a secondary attachment figure and correspondingly less help.

Who would your pup rather play with, you or another dog? If it is *not* you, you need to increase the amount of *quality* time you spend with your pup. One to one play, without another dog.

We have another slight issue with attachment because it is yet another source of income for Pet Behaviour Counsellors. Well, not actually attachment itself, but rather over-attachment. Attachment is fine, over-attachment is not.

Attachment is a good process when it starts with mum, because it allows infants a secure base from which to explore in safety, but we do a strange thing with our pups. At exactly the time when mum is weaning them off her, both physically and emotionally, we adopt them. Mum is actively encouraging them to be independent and we encourage them to be dependent upon us. We cuddle them, feed them and lavish care and attention on them, preventing them from developing any self-reliance.

For us, the importance of our primary attachment figures can change over time; your mum becomes less important as you leave home. Not so for dogs. Dogs are behaviourally frozen in adolescence in comparison to wild canids like the wolf. In non-domesticated species juvenile behaviour is very malleable and adult behaviour is relatively fixed. In domesticated species, like the dog, we actually *want* them to remain attached and we breed them specifically for the trait ("Aww, Satan loves his Daddy"). This means that dogs as a species retain the need for a primary attachment figure in a way that wolves don't.

Okay, up to a point this is why we have puppies. But what is the difference between attachment, which will happen anyway, and over-attachment, which we want to avoid? The problems can begin when we start to do some of that socialising we talked about. If we get it wrong (to err *is* human...) and the puppy is frightened, she needs to do something to reduce that fear. Hiding behind an attachment figure is a good coping strategy; it makes puppy feel more secure. And, truth be told, we quite like protecting our puppy. It stirs parental instincts in us.

But are we doing our pup any favours? Well, if pup can only cope with stress when we are there, what happens when we are not? If the pup becomes so attached to us that she can't cope with the slightest challenge without us, how will she feel when we are not there? Now even when we *are* there, she is going to worry that we will leave. All her emotional well-being depends on us being there. Not a good picture for emotional development, but how do we prevent it?

Not too difficult, actually. We need to encourage her to take enjoyment from other people, to reduce the idea that all good things only come from us, and we need to make sure that we don't try to do too much *scary* socialising.

I know that sounds like the opposite of what I said about getting plenty of socialisation, but it isn't. It is about the quality of the socialisation. If the experiences you provide for your pup are *not* scary, they will generalise into her maintenance set without worrying her. If the experiences you provide *are* scary, she will have to find a way of coping, and that is likely to be depending upon you. Too many daunting experiences and she is in deep emotional trouble.

So, whilst it is good to show her the world, it has to be in a non-threatening way. There are theories that suggest that too much socialisation encourages over-attachment. What they fail to take into account is the quality of the socialisation. Too much *poor quality* socialisation will scare your puppy and make her look for comfort. Good quality socialisation does not lead to over-attachment.

But, but, but... what do we do when we *do* get it wrong and accidentally introduce our pup to a scary experience? She has to learn to cope, but she also needs some back-up. Who better than her primary attachment figure, who she can look to for advice on how to act?

For starters, just being there will help, but don't go overboard. Don't mollycoddle her, don't do the, "There, there, there, Mummy will make it all better, then..." scoop up and cuddle. Just march confidently through daily life and pup will take her cue from you. "Nothing's a problem, 'cos Mum's not bothered". Or you can do the "jolly uncle" act: laugh heartily and walk on past the problem assertively, a bit like Baloo the bear in the Jungle Book. Laughing at problems is a much better coping strategy than depending on Mum for your emotional stability.

Now we're developing a puppy that looks forward to new experiences and laughs in the face of problems. Not a bad start, I think, but where do we go from here? Like the laws of gravity, the laws of learning are never switched off. Our pups are learning all the time, so we need to make sure that *what* they are learning is what we want, or they'll fill in the gaps themselves. The next chapter will give direction to that learning by pointing them in the right direction with the creative use of toys and games.

Chapter Nine

Toys and Games

The Secret Way to a Dog's Heart

Toys and games? Have we gone soft? This is supposed to be a book about dog training; hard facts about justifiable training methods, not namby-pamby, wishy-washy, touchy-feely playing around with toys and games. Agreed, and this chapter will be no different. You could call it "behavioural modulation through the expression of each individual's inherited predispositions to ensure compatibility with owner expectations", but the way we do that is through the games our dogs play and the toys that they play with, and I think "Toys and Games" is a bit more user-friendly.

Technically, "play" is regarded as being the non-functional display of adult motor patterns, either truncated or out of context and is most often seen in juvenile animals. Breaking that down a bit, a "motor pattern" is a piece of an inherited behaviour that the dog enjoys performing. How about the "mouse-pounce" I mentioned in Chapter Two as an example? It is part of a food gathering process that goes something like this...

Our undomesticated canid hears a mouse in the long grass and fixes her stare on the exact spot. Her ears are up and forwards, to catch every sound, neck arched to see above the grass and her whole face is tensed in anticipatory concentration. She leaps upwards in a graceful arc, like a show-jumper clearing a high wall, propelled by supple thigh muscles, tail out as her rudder. She hangs in the air for a microsecond then lands, her whole weight transferred to her front legs, stretched stiffly below her like a stotting antelope, on top of the hapless rodent. Trapped by her front paws and either dead or stunned, the snack is quickly consumed.

Dogs use the same motor pattern in play but it is not directed towards its proper target, live food. Instead, like kittens with a ball of wool, they perform it on alternative targets such as leaves or shadows on the lino, so that makes it "out of context". Consequently it is frequently not carried right through from start to finish, "truncated", as there is no snack to pick up at the end of it. It is "non-functional" *because* there is no snack at the end of it; it is performed just for the sake of it, rather than the function of satisfying hunger.

As a motor pattern, it is instinctive, not learnt. She simply knows how to do it and always has done. In the wild, animals that practice these kind of motor patterns will be more successful when they have to perform them for real, and that is what play is all about.

Whilst you are young, you are looked after by Mum and Dad, and consequently have spare time on your hands. If you use that spare time to practice motor patterns that you will use when you grow up, you will be better at them when you really need to be, that is, when you are on your own and hungry. Therefore most play is seen in juvenile animals; old enough to act like a grown-up but young enough to still be taken care of.

We already know that dogs are trapped in permanent adolescence as a consequence of the self-domestication process, so it should come as no surprise that dogs play all their lives. Wolves and foxes grow out of it when they mature; life is too serious to play when you're living paw to mouth. But dogs never grow out of playing; they play their whole lives. Yet another reason we love them so much.

Incidentally, there are very few examples of animals that play extensively when adults, but humans do – yet another reason why we enjoy our dogs.

Have you noticed that the hunting motor patterns are the ones that have been selectively enhanced or reduced in different breeds of dogs? We looked at it back in Chapter Three when we investigated what breeds are and why they developed. Our domesticated working dogs are *playing* because they are performing the behaviour without it resulting in the original function.

Now we know what play is, it makes it easier to recognise and understand how important it is for our dogs. Any inherited motor pattern that doesn't result in its original canine function is play. Labradors bringing back pheasants and not eating them must be playing. Greyhounds chasing a dummy bunny round a track must be playing. Spaniels sniffing out drugs at an airport must be playing. Bloodhounds tracking down criminals must be playing. Border Collies rounding up sheep must be playing. Corgis nipping my heels must be playing. All hunting motor patterns that don't achieve the final outcome of eating are play. Likewise, all mating motor patterns that don't aim at procreation are also play (you always knew that Trixie was humping the vicar's leg just for fun, didn't you?)

Time to see what we've got so far:

- Dogs originally bred for a specific purpose are playing.
- They do it for the huge boost of feel-good factor from their brain chemistry when they perform their breed specific role.
- They enjoy it so much they are driven to perform it; they *need* to do it.
- Most dogs are pets.
- Pets don't have the opportunity to work-off their breed specific behaviours by performing their original role.

Hmm, seems like a problem might be developing here. It would appear that Collies with no sheep to herd must be miserable, Labradors with no pheasants to pick up must be depressed and Jack Russell Terriers with no rats to shake must be despondent. They are deprived of the opportunity to gain that fix of dopamine that sends the endorphins whizzing round their bodies making them feel *so alive!*

And, if that were the end of the story, it would be true; they would lead a truly sad life. Luckily, it isn't the end. They are playing when they herd sheep, pick up birds and shake rats. Their behaviour is truncated and out of context. But, like the kittens with a ball of wool, the target

205

of that behaviour is not important in order for them to take enjoyment from performing it.

It matters hugely *that* Collies herd, Labradors pick up and Terriers shake for them to lead fulfilled lives, but it doesn't matter *what* Collies herd, Labradors pick up and Terriers shake. They can take the same fulfilment from playing games with toys. Look at them as puppies: Collie pups will herd children or the family cat, Labrador pups will pick up slippers or tissues and Terrier pups will shake socks or your trouser leg.

The last chapter was about puppy development and so is this one; it is about growing the behaviour of our puppy by pointing her in the right direction. Even when we first adopt them, as eight-week-old pups, our dogs are starting to show breed specific preferences. If we leave them alone, they will find ways of exhibiting their breed behaviours. Anything that moves will be chased, things left lying around will be picked up and carried around or shaken to destruction. If we leave puppies alone they will find a way to be herders, carriers and shakers. They will decide what to herd, carry and chase. Why would we leave such an important decision to an eight-week-old puppy?

Let me explain. I'll use "chase" again, as most dogs like to chase, at least a little bit. Our dog is rewarded inside with a "buzz", like we get when we score a goal, each time she chases something. Now, originally, the "thing" that she would have been chasing was probably something small and furry, and the whole predatory sequence ended in lunch. The "catch, kill and eat" part reinforced not only the chasing, but also *what* she chased. But our dogs don't live like that any more. Yes, okay, their brains are probably still set up to find small furry things very attractive to chase, hence all the trouble people have with rabbit chasers, but they can find chasing something else just as rewarding.

We're back into "neuroscience made simple" again. There is a little part of our dog's brain that is captioned "chasing is good", so she casts around for something to chase. There are lots of possibilities; let's use cars, sheep, rabbits and tennis balls as examples. Every time she chases a car, there is a join made between the "chase" part of her brain and the "cars" part. Likewise joins are made between "chase" and "sheep", "chase" and "rabbits" and "chase" and "tennis balls" each time they are used as a target for the "chasing is good" centre.

This establishes preferences in her mind. If she's chased cars 100 times, sheep 50 times, rabbits 20 times and tennis balls 10 times, and all four appear in front of her at the same time, she will prefer to chase the car. This dog prefers to chase rabbits over tennis balls, sheep over them both and cars most of all. It is simple maths. The more she aims her "chasing is good" behaviour at a particular target, the more reinforcing it becomes. It is an easy step from, "I feel good when I chase cars" to get to, "To feel good I must chase cars."

The other targets will do if there are no cars about, but the most used target is preferred. This is slightly over-simplified, as there are probably hard wired preferences too, for example small furry things are more interesting to chase than stones, so it isn't exactly proportionate. Nobody has done any scientific experiments, as each dog will be different, so I don't know the precise figures, but it is likely that to make a stone a preferred target over a rabbit you will have to make a lot more joins between the "chase" and "stone" than the "chase" and "rabbit" brain centres. However, the principle holds.

Have you noticed anything about the targets I have listed up to now? The only one we have control over is the tennis ball. Cars, rabbits, sheep and even stones can be chosen at random by our dog, as can cats, children, other dogs, birds, cyclists, joggers, leaves, shadows, flies and anything else found at large in the environment.

If we have any aspirations to control our dog, we have to control the things she finds important, remember? There isn't any way we can control things at large in the environment, like cars, sheep or rabbits, so if it is very important to our dog that she chases one of those, we have no control over her. If we allow her to choose her own primary chase target we are relinquishing control of her behaviour.

Remember Flash the Border Collie that chased aeroplanes, back in Chapter Three? Now perhaps you can appreciate how much effort we had to put into getting him to change his chase target to a Frisbee. He was so wired to aeroplanes! It would have been much easier to establish a preference we could control from the start, rather than changing one he chose himself, but with some dogs we just don't have that option.

What to do with our pup? Easy, *we* choose her primary chase target. How to do it? Also easy: from the day she first starts to want to chase something, we direct that behaviour towards something we find appropriate. Play chase with a tennis ball, or other toy, from the start and she will like to chase tennis balls more than anything else.

This gives us a tremendous edge in controlling her behaviour. Want to chase something? I've got it. Behave nicely and you can chase it. Bring it back and you can chase it again.

Training interlude…. "How to get your dog to fetch"…

There are three main methods, so I'll give you them in ascending order. Start with the first and if it doesn't work, move on to the second, then the third if that doesn't work. If the third fails, combine the latter two to make a fourth method. There are *four* main methods…

In all cases, don't speak to your dog if she is doing it wrong and give her effusive feedback praise if she is doing it right. Remember the training rules: start in a place with no distractions to acquire and then become fluent, to avoid confusion. If you start in a big outside area she has too many options other than bringing the ball back to you. If you start in a small indoor area her options are severely limited.

Now, we already know that individual's, as well as different breeds', desire to retrieve will not all be the same because of inherited breed specific effects, so we need to have different strategies depending upon how keen our dog is to perform the whole behaviour. One size training does not fit all.

First method: The "Lazy Bones". Throw the ball and then wait until our pup brings it back. Act like you are not interested. When pup nudges you with the ball, take it like it is the best gift ever and immediately throw it again. Repeat. Works for pups that *really* want to retrieve.

Second method: The "Grass is Always Greener". Throw the ball and as pup picks it up, immediately turn your back and play with a second, identical ball. It has to be identical because the only difference in value it should have for our pup is the fact that she doesn't actually have this one. Kneel down and play gently with the second ball by yourself. Pup will not be able to resist coming to see, and will probably drop the first ball when she gets close. Immediately reward the dropping of the first ball with a throw of the second ball. Then pick up the first, turn your back and repeat. It will work better if you are able to throw in alternate directions, so pup has to pass you with one ball in order to anticipate the next throw. Works for pups that like to chase more than pick up and return with it.

Third method: The "Gentle Touch". First tie a length of curtain cord to pup's collar. The length will depend upon the environment you are working in, but shouldn't need to be more than ten feet indoors. Throw the ball and wait until pup picks it up. Call pup *once* then gently but silently reel her in, hand over hand with the cord. This is not a fight, just an inevitable outcome, like the changing of the seasons. When she arrives, gently take the ball and immediately throw it again. Repeat as necessary. Works for pups that like to chase but are reluctant to come back.

Fourth method: The "Combined Effort". Combine the "Grass is Always Greener" with the "Gentle Touch" by using the cord to get her in close, then showing her that the second ball is more attractive. Never fight your pup for the ball in her mouth. Take hold of it firmly and play with the second ball in front of her until she lets go of the first. Always reward the dropping or leaving of one ball with the throw of another. Works for pups that don't like to give the ball back.

In all of these examples we must reward giving the ball up with another throw immediately, either with the fetched ball or another identical one.

You will notice that in none of the examples do we move towards the pup. Why not chase her into a corner and take the ball from her? Two reasons: Firstly, being chased is at least as good a game as fetching, but one which she can control, so let's not teach her that one. Secondly she is likely to become either frightened at being cornered, or determined to defend her prize, either of which can result in an aggressive response as we approach. Let's definitely not teach her that game!

The emphasis on training is control. Not of the pup, but of the circumstances. Plan the situation so that the inevitable outcome is that she brings the ball. My ideal retrieve location is a corridor devoid of furniture. I sit in the middle and throw the ball. As she brings it back (she has nowhere else to go) I reward her with a throw of the second ball in the other direction.

The next bit is up to you. You can refine your pup's retrieve in any way you like. If you want her to drop the ball at your feet, tempt her with a second ball until, overcome with desire, she drops the first. Immediately throw the second; it is operant conditioning so get the reinforcer (ball throw) in as quickly as you can!

If you think about it, the traditional way of teaching a retrieve is to throw a ball and demand that pup brings it back. Pup is in a position of control for a moment when she decides whether or not to comply. I want the word "Leave" to predict a gain, not a loss, so say "Leave" as you throw the second ball. That way the word predicts the arrival of the new ball. Your pup will leave the first one for the second, and "Leave" predicts that they will win a resource, not lose one. Retrieve training is continually positive, rather than being punctuated by small losses. Pup will associate leaving what she has with gaining something better.

213

If you want her to hold on to the ball until you take it, keep the second ball in your pocket and, when you both have a grip on the first, say, "leave" and produce it with a flourish like a rabbit from a top hat. The word "leave" will come to predict the production of a second ball so she will want to let go of the first.

Trainers see the progression as in increase in the three Ds: Difficulty, Duration and Distraction. The Difficulty increases as you throw it further, the Duration as you increase the number of throws and Distraction when you make the environment more complicated (up to and including when there are other chase targets about, like in the park). Never try to do all three at once. If you are increasing Duration, keep Difficulty and Distraction the same; if you are increasing Difficulty, keep the other two the same; if you... well, I'm sure you've got the picture: just one thing at a time.

Training interlude over, let's get back to the bigger picture.

That was an example of how to play one game, retrieving, with our pup. What teaching the retrieve does for us is to give us control over our pup's primary chase target; the thing she would rather chase than anything else. Because the game is so rewarding for her, we can actually use it as a reward for giving up other, less appropriate behaviour. "Don't do *that*, come here instead and as a reward, play *this*!"

The offer of a game can be made conditional on any behaviour you choose. "Sit on that mat until the visitors have gone and we will play the game". This is sometimes called "Grandma's Rule" which goes along the somewhat less than scientific lines of, "If you eat your cabbage, you can have some pudding".

Our pup's preferred behaviour of retrieving (pudding) reinforces the less preferred behaviour of sitting quietly (cabbage).

The spin-offs from retrieving are rich and varied:

- We get a recall: she has to come back to play the game.
- We get a "leave" or "drop" command: she will give up stuff she has "accidentally" borrowed.
- We can play "tug of war" because we have a "leave" command.
- We get searching: essential for searching breeds like spaniels to work off their need to search (for something that we control). Throw the ball into longer grass and pup will naturally search for it.
- We get a nice relationship with our pup because she likes to play games we control.

    And this is just from one game!

What other games can we play that might be useful? How about another dead easy one: the recall game?

Training interlude…"How to teach your dog to come back."

Take one dog, two people and a high value reinforcer. A high value reinforcer will either be top quality food or the above mentioned ball, depending upon your dog's individual preferences. When I say, "top quality food" I don't necessarily mean beluga caviar, but something your dog really likes. Ordinary dog nosh will not do. If I asked you to get up and switch off the TV, would you do it for a chip? No, but you might for something you find really special, like a cake?

By the way, this is a great game for children to join in as well. As this is dog training we are going to start in a place with no distractions. The three of you start in the front room with the treats shared equally between the two people, but out of sight in pockets.

First person holds pup by the collar and second shows her a treat going into the pocket, before running away into the kitchen. Second person calls the chosen word, ("come", "here", whatever… the word itself doesn't matter as much as the consistency in using it).

Puppy pulls on the collar to get away and first person allows her to go. She scampers into the kitchen to find second person waiting for her.

This is the important bit. Second person *takes hold of pup's collar* and then delivers her treat from their pocket.

Second person now has puppy by the collar and first person calls pup from the front room. Repeat as necessary. Always hold the collar to make sure pup comes right back before rewarding with the treat or retrieve game.

Progress by:

- Going further away.
- Hiding: it makes a great game of hide and seek!
- Phasing out the sausage in the easier hiding places, remember variable ratio reinforcement?
- Introducing distractions: play the game on walks.

What if you are on your own? Probably not as much fun, but one idea is to train the end result and let the dog do the work.

For "recall" it goes like this. Arrange for your dog to be sitting in front of you, touch her collar and say your recall word, before reinforcing her with her high value reward. If you do this enough times she will realise that when you say the word and touch her collar, she gets a big reward. When you say the word in future, she knows she only has to have her collar touched to earn a reward. It sounds simple, but it works. Provided the reinforcer is sufficiently high value, she will work hard to earn it by coming back. Train it using the usual rules for dog training: start in a place with no distractions, phase out the reinforcer and so on.

Herman was a Vizla with attitude. At dog training class Paul, his owner, told me that he would never come back when called.

"How do you manage to catch him, then?" I asked, imagining things like Paul leaping onto Herman from behind a bush, or feigning unconsciousness and nabbing him when he came to investigate.

"Oh, easy," was the reply, "I just tell him to sit."

"Ah, then you walk up and clip him on?"

"No, look." And Paul let Herman off his lead. When he was fifty feet away, Paul quietly said, "Sit", and Herman flew back, thumping to the floor in front of him, in a textbook recall. "But if I call him, he won't come," complained Paul. I explained that Herman had learned the recall the easy way. He knew that if he sat in front when asked, he got a reward. He just hadn't learned that the same applied when Paul called, "Here". Sometimes I think our dogs train themselves despite us, rather than because of us.

What do recall games get you? A dog that is happy to come back. How much is that worth? You decide.

Training interlude over again... back to toys and games...

Okay, so we've looked at two simple games that all dogs can play, but we know that dog behaviour is breed specific, so the games they play will develop along breed lines, too. What can we do about that? Well, there are so many different breeds it would be impossible to list all the possibilities in this book, but we can generalise our original examples: Border Collies, Labradors and Jack Russell Terriers, into "herders", "fetchers" and "terriers".

If you have a dog of a breed originally designed to herd, to determine the kinds of game your dog will like, you need to ask, "What do herders like to do?" The answer is in the question, really, "herd", and that breaks down into chasing, circling and catching.

Already we know we are dealing with some kind of object that our herder wants to use some herding behaviour on, so that's a good start. If it is small, like a tennis ball, she can certainly chase and catch, but if it is bigger, like a football, she can also run around it. If it hovers in the air, like a Frisbee, our herder can chase, run around it, and then catch it. You can also buy especially big, un-burstable balls that she can't get her teeth into, if she is a football shredder.

"Fetchers" usually also want to search, so you'll be playing searching games. Show her a ball whilst somebody else holds her collar (as in "Recall Game") and pretend to hide it in three different places in the front room, whilst she watches. Let her go and see her search! Top Tip: don't hide it in places that she needs to destroy to find it. Down the back of the sofa is definitely out, unless you want torn cushions!

Take the game out on walks, or simply throw the toy into long grass for her to sniff out. Remember she will be using her nose, so the wind needs to be blowing from the toy towards her for her to be able to find it.

If you want to play the game but your dog isn't a fetcher or particularly motivated by toys, you could do the same with a food treat, allowing her to eat it as the reward.

Terriers? What are terriers for? Well, sorry to puncture the cosy bubble but terriers are born to go down holes and kill small furry animals. On the plus side, this gives them lots of opportunities for games. Terriers love to play ragging, you know, that manic shake of the head from side to side, with almost any soft toy. Now there's a motor pattern! They'll also chase and grab, which means we've got the start of a retrieve.

What about digging? We've got two alternative styles of digging. The first is the "going to earth" type, where they dive into burrows. Holes and warrens can be simulated in a garden adventure playground using water-main pipe if you can afford (or scrounge) it, or cardboard boxes if you can't. The second type is actual scratching at the earth and dislodging clods of it in all directions. Lots of behaviour consultations begin, "How can I stop my dog digging up my (flowerbeds, carpets, lawns, bulbs...?)". The answer is not to stop terriers digging, but to give them a legitimate outlet for it. Build a "bark-pit"; like a sandpit only filled with forest bark. Let your terrier see you burying some tasty treats in it and let her go. Once she realises that digging here is more rewarding that digging anywhere else, she won't bother with the rest of the garden!

Mrs Featherstone's three lovely miniature dachshunds, Brandy, Sherry and little Port, were digging up her lawn. I discovered that they made such a mess with their food she had taken to feeding them outside, in the garden. Although they usually picked up all the pieces, occasionally one would escape and lodge in the grass, making it a great place to pick up treats later.

After we changed their feeding place from the grass to the patio, occasionally some food now lodges in between the flags. They've stopped digging the lawn and now she gets her patio weeded for free. In fact, when she spends the afternoon weeding, drops some treats on the patio and they all join in together!

If you don't have a herder, fetcher or terrier, you need to think about how your dog's behaviour can be represented in games. Think, adapt, and be inventive. At the very least there are a range of food-playing toys on the market designed to stimulate your dog's mind even when you are not there.

And finally, on toys and games, some dog owners will be wondering what all this fuss is about. These are the ones whose dogs don't have a big drive to exhibit any breed specific behaviour, or show low activity levels. In fact, some dogs are actually bred to like sitting around all day, for example, the sheep guarders. Great. Relax, lie back and enjoy your dog. But you are in the minority. For the rest of us, our dogs need other outlets for their behaviour to maintain their emotional homeostasis. Emotional homeostasis? Yes, indeed, treading where angels fear, our next foray is into the contentious issue of our dogs' emotions.

Chapter Ten
Dogs Have Emotions Too!

The Secret of a Happy Dog

For centuries scientists have argued over whether animals have emotions like ours. The French 17th Century philosopher and all round great thinker, Rene Descartes ("I think, therefore I am") formed a school of thought that the human mind was the also the soul. As animals did not have a soul, they had no experience of "mind" and so could not feel even pain, let alone emotions! On the other hand, the belief systems of all kinds of hunter-gatherers, from Alaskan Inuit to Australian aboriginals, all endow animals with emotions at least the same as ours, and sometimes more.

Of course, we all *know* that our dogs experience emotions, because we live with them and observe them daily, but that is not empirical proof. Descartes lived with them and observed them, too. The problem is that we cannot examine exactly what the dog is feeling and compare it with what we know we feel. Confusion can arise because it is part of the human condition to believe that other people can feel the same way we do. We want to project our emotions onto others, but unfortunately it can be a mistake to do this with non-human things.

Even when we know it isn't possible, we attribute feelings to inanimate objects, like traffic lights. I regularly complain that they have turned to red just because they saw me coming! For goodness sake, people give names to cars, "Ah, good old Bertha never lets me down." And Basil Fawlty famously thrashed his to teach it a lesson!

Assigning human qualities to animals can be a huge source of misunderstanding, as illustrated by the story of Clever Hans. In 1907 Herr Von Osten, a German gentleman, taught his horse, Hans, to tap out the answers to mathematical questions. When asked, "What is 2 + 2?" Hans would give four taps of his hoof, only the questions were much tougher, and in German. It wasn't a con, because Von Osten truly believed the horse was calculating for himself, but others were more sceptical.

If it had been a fairy tale, the king would have offered his daughter's hand in marriage to anyone in the land who could tell how the horse was doing it but, as it was in Germany, they set up a commission of prominent scientists who devised a series of experiments instead.

Oskar Pfungst, the author of the tale, was able to establish that the right answer did not depend on the difficulty of the question, like it would with me. Hans got the answer right if two, and only two, conditions were fulfilled. Firstly, that the person asking the question knew the answer and secondly that Hans could see that person.

It turned out that Hans was picking up on the minute changes in tension in the body language of the questioner as the right answer approached, stopping on the almost invisible cues given off with the release of tension at the right number. It didn't have to be Von Osten, anyone would do and sometimes even when they knew what was happening and tried to not give off clues, Hans was *still* able to tell!

Hans had learned to keep going until the tension relaxed, a simple example of operant conditioning. Believing that Hans really was clever and could do complicated maths was a contravention of the scientific

'Principle of Parsimony', also called 'Lloyd-Morgan's Canon' or 'Occam's Razor'.

Morgan formulated a law (canon) in 1907 that said, "In no case is an animal activity to be interpreted in terms of higher psychological processes, if it can be fairly interpreted in terms of processes which stand lower in the scale of psychological evolution and development." William of Ockham said something similar in Latin in the 1300s, but he probably nicked it from somebody else before him as well. This all sounds a bit like the offside rule in terms of ease of understanding, but it boils down to: "If anything can be explained by a simple process, it is wrong to assign a more complicated reason."

We have to be careful when attributing human qualities to animals. Here's a doggy example to make it clearer:

Janet wanted to know how to stop Barney leaving a large smelly deposit on the best Wilton when she was at work. Barney was a three year-old Labrador. He had been adopted from a rescue society just over a year before, because, although Janet had a lot of time for a dog, she also had to leave him at home for four hours during the day. Barney was well housetrained and had no 'accidents' in the previous twelve months, but then it all went wrong.

For three weeks, every night when she came home Barney had dumped on the carpet. In her own words, "He knows he's done wrong – he looks so guilty when I come in. Now he even hides!" Janet was convinced that Barney felt guilty, until we discussed how this "guilty" look developed.

The first time Barney had pooped, Janet came home and got her normal greeting, which consisted of Barney hurling himself at her, tongue slobbering and tail wagging. When she got past the effusive greeting, she saw and smelled the offending heap and exclaimed, "What have you done?" in a voice any drill sergeant would be proud of. This was followed by shutting Barney outside whilst she cleaned up the mess, muttering, clattering and stomping as she tried to return the carpet to its former glory. Eventually she let Barney back in, but she was a bit cheesed off at having her carpet ruined and pretty much ignored him for the rest of the night, rather than the usual cuddles on her knee.

The next evening Janet was a bit apprehensive about what she might find when she returned home and didn't call out her usual cheery, "Hello Barney, Mummy's home!" as she opened the door. Barney didn't greet her normally, either. He sidled towards her, licking his lips, ears flat, tail tucked under, eyes half closed. As the smell assaulted her nostrils Janet thundered, "What have you done?" again, and Barney headed for the door to escape her wrath. Sure enough, a large pile of do-dos decorated the floor. This was repeated on successive days, with more and more 'guilt', until Barney just hid when she came home. "Why does he do it if he knows he's done wrong?" she exclaimed.

Does he know he's done wrong? Look at it from Barney's point of view. Barney pooped. He could have done it for a number of reasons, from a car backfiring in the street outside to a gastro-intestinal upset, but when he did it, it felt good. It was a relief from the pressure of a full bowel. Have you ever been caught short and been dying for the loo? How good does it feel when you finally get that blessed relief? Let's just say it was an enjoyable experience. Barney felt better for having pooped. Pooping on the carpet was nice.

The first time Janet came home, Barney had no idea he was in trouble for pooping; in fact he probably didn't even remember doing it, he was so overcome with excitement at Mum coming home. What happened afterwards was a huge shock. Yelled at, shut out and ignored for the rest of the night. Mum in a foul mood was a very nasty experience, but he had nothing to connect it to. He didn't know why. All he knew was that when Mum came home things got really bad. This was a huge learning event for him. He wouldn't forget it easily.

The next night when he heard the car in the driveway, he started to become anxious. Would it be trouble again? He must be on high alert for anything out of the ordinary. Oh dear, Mum didn't act normally when she opened the door. How can he fend off any impending conflict? Appeasement: he approached gingerly, licking his lips, ears flat, tail tucked under, eyes half closed; converting all his body language into "Don't hurt me, I mean no harm, can we be friends?" gestures.

But that didn't work and she went ballistic again, so he legged it. When Janet saw Barney's different body language and smelled the poop, she put two and two together and decided that he must be showing guilt. After all, if a person had done something like that they would have acted guilty!

What Janet couldn't have known is that even if Barney *hadn't* pooped on the second day, he would have acted the same. He wasn't feeling guilty, just worried about Janet's arrival being as scary as it had been the previous night. The fact that he *had* pooped reinforced Janet's belief that he must be showing guilt. Oh, yes, conditioning works on people too!

Each day Barney was more and more anxious about Janet coming home, so each night Janet's arrival was more and more scary, and definitely to be avoided. Barney made no association between taking a dump and her mood. How could he, when they were three hours apart?

Do dogs feel guilt? There is absolutely no evidence for it. Why was Barney pooping and how to stop him? We'll return to that later, but it involves that 'emotional homeostasis' I mentioned.

But if dogs don't feel guilt, what emotions do they feel? We already decided they *do* attach to significant others, which in humans would be called "love" or at least, "affection", so there is evidence for some emotions comparable to ours, but how do we know where to stop? How do we know which emotions to include and which ones to exclude? "Love" is in but "guilt" is out. What about jealousy, happiness, sadness, frustration, anger, elation, fear, anticipation, disappointment, embarrassment, pride, shame, remorse, contempt, humiliation, sympathy, compassion?

Well, everything listed up to 'disappointment' is probably in and everything after it is probably out, and here's why. Species don't develop anything without a reason.

What are emotions for? How would they help canines survive to produce other canines with the same emotions? What use are they in the genetic survival sense? How would a dog with emotions be better able to pass on her genes than a dog without emotions?

In view of the principle of parsimony, and to get away from the whole emotional aspect of emotions, in animals they have been called positive and negative motivational affective states, but as far as I am concerned there is no difference between motivational affective states and emotions. Not surprisingly, they serve to improve the chances of genetic survival.

Negative motivational affective states/ emotions arise when an animal needs to remove itself from a problem of some sort and they drive it to seek a solution. It's a negative state, so something aversive; it's motivational, so it encourages some sort of action; and affective just means emotional.

If your body lacks water, the negative motivational state of 'thirst' makes you go out and buy a bottle of Evian, or slurp rain from a puddle, depending upon where (or what) you are. In the same way, a dog that is experiencing the negative motivational affective state (emotion) of 'loneliness' might howl to try to call Mum back home, or maybe try to dig through the door to get out.

Negative emotions serve to make us feel we have to change the circumstances we find ourselves in. Frustration makes us try harder; fear can make us run or hide, anger makes us want to fight; jealousy makes us want to protect what we hold dear.

Positive motivational affective states (what the heck, let's just call them 'emotions') arise when an animal performs an action that will have a long term genetic benefit, such as social interaction, or play. The benefit may not be immediately obvious, but the pleasure derived from performing it is enough to encourage the animal. That way, the pleasure of *playing* 'mouse-pounce' is reflected in a greater competence at catching mice later in life, so she can eat, survive and reproduce.

Positive emotions make us feel good when we do things that may have no immediate benefit. Affection makes us want to hang around those we love because in the long term having a family has genetic benefits; anticipation makes us stay around for long enough to collect the nice thing that is going to happen; elation makes us want to repeat what we did; happiness makes us want to remain in the situation for as long as we can.

The function of canine emotions is to make dogs act either to remove a negative feeling, or acquire a positive one. The feelings are linked to actions that have genetic benefits in either taking away trouble or adding opportunity. If emotions are so beneficial then, why the cut-off from embarrassment, pride, shame, remorse, contempt, humiliation, sympathy and compassion? The difference is that all these emotions need empathy, and empathy needs self-awareness.

Despite a huge amount of experiments, no one has ever found any evidence for a human level of self-awareness in dogs. It can be best described as a lack of knowing about oneself. Dogs feel that they are doing something, but they don't know that they feel it. Hmm, a bit confusing, eh? How about instead of, "I think, therefore I am," dogs are more, "I feel, therefore I do."

Imagine your drive to work. Usually you pay complete attention to the road and are aware of what you are doing all of the time. Just occasionally though, you'll pull into the car park and realise that you have been so lost in thought that you have absolutely no recollection of having driven the last five miles. Yet you've obviously negotiated roundabouts, traffic lights and one-way systems, or you couldn't have arrived safely. You did it, but you weren't aware of doing it. It seems that this is how dogs live their lives; responding, but not *knowing* they are responding. Dogs *experience* emotions, but they can't step outside the feeling and look inwards to know *that* they are feeling happy. If they can't look inside and *know* they are experiencing happiness, they can't look at us and speculate on what we are feeling either.

Without awareness of themselves, dogs cannot make the huge leap to putting themselves in our place, to empathise with our feelings. Sure, they know when we are in a bad (or good) mood, but they can't put themselves in our place to understand what that mood feels like. They can't speculate, "If I do this it will make Mum feel like this." To be embarrassed they need to know that we know what they know; to be proud, or ashamed, or remorseful, or sympathetic they have to envisage how we would feel in order to respond to it.

"But my dog knows when I'm angry (sad/happy/etc)".

Yes, agreed, she does. Because of the effect on her. But she doesn't know *what* you are experiencing. She knows that when you have *that* expression, when you give off *that* body language, that certain things happen as a result. It's classical conditioning: frowns and harsh words go together; smiles and extra treats go together. Any emotion that requires dogs to put themselves in the place of another is not possible.

Okay so far, but what has this got to do with dog training? The fact is that we cannot separate training a dog from her emotions; how we train, what we train and, in the case of Janet and Barney, even why we train. Training and living with a dog is an emotional experience for them as well as us.

If you yell at a dog until she sits, what emotion does she associate with training? If you lift a treat above her head until she sits then drop it into her mouth how do you think she feels about training?

Training is all about emotions, for example puppies at my puppy class often have to be carried in (we hold them at veterinary surgeries) for the first week or two. We need to be aware of their emotions and vary our training accordingly. Some pups don't do anything at all at the start, just sit there taking it all in whilst their emotions cope with the new experience. By the third or fourth week they are often towing their owners behind them, they are so eager to come in. The change in their emotions makes all the difference. Can you train an anxious, worried, apprehensive puppy? Not very easily. Can you train a happy puppy that is looking forward to some fun? You betcha!

And, at long last, this is where "homeostasis" comes in. From the Greek, homo = 'the same' and stasis = 'to stand', it translates as "standing the same" and is used to describe our bodies' need to remain in a stable state.

I'll give you an example. Human bodies work best at a temperature of 98.6° F (37° C) give or take a degree or so, depending upon whom you ask. Much more than that and we overheat, in fact at a body temperature of 104° we begin to get major organ failure and at 106°, brain death from hyperthermia. Much less than 95° and our metabolism turns to sludge, to the extent that at about 90° we start to die from hypothermia. We're only ever six or eight degrees away from death.

Consequently, our bodies are constantly monitoring and adjusting our temperature, working towards that point of temperature homeostasis of 98.6°F. If we heat up, we start to sweat and blood is sent to vessels nearer the surface to cool down. If we cool down too much our blood is diverted to core organs, away from the extremities, and we shiver, converting muscle action to heat.

Most of the time this is going on we aren't even aware of it, but our body is continually fine-tuning to keep itself running at exactly the right temperature for optimum performance. That way we are better able to survive to reproduce.

A similar system works for our emotions. Emotional homeostasis may be a little more complicated than temperature regulation, but the principle is exactly the same. If we were constantly angry or frustrated or even euphoric, we would not be able to function to our optimum performance, so we need to keep our overall positive and negative emotions in balance.

The mid-point of emotional homeostasis will be slightly different for different individuals, I'm sure we all know someone who is "only happy when he's miserable", but we all have one, and our bodies are constantly striving to be at or just above it. It is the point at which we feel okay. Not fantastic or terrible, but the "okay" that we expect people to use as the answer to, "How are you?"

If you are feeling terrible or fantastic, your body can't sustain that for very long and works towards balancing emotional homeostasis. In the case of "fantastic" all that happens is that the system supporting the feeling degenerates, leaving us with the desire to do it again. In the case of "terrible" our body works to get us out of the state that made us like that. As with most other things, these feelings are manipulated by brain chemistry, but the results are positive and negative emotions.

We need to be aware of our dogs' emotional needs if they are going to live a happy life. Everyday living constantly provides challenges to dogs' emotional homeostasis. Every time the post drops through the letterbox her stress levels go up as she defends us all by driving the Posty away. When low flying planes, fireworks, or things that go bump in the night scare her, she goes into negative emotions of fear and possibly anxiety. She needs to be able to cope with these challenges.

Dogs have three normal, genetically prepared, ways to cope with fear. These are hiding, running away and fighting. All three strategies are capable of removing a scary threat. Hide and it won't see you. Run away and it can't catch you. Fight and you make it retreat.

Hiding and running away can't work for the Posty, because our dog is in the safest place there is: home. But fighting works every time. Bark like mad and the Posty runs away, after posting the mail. And it works every day. Every day millions of dogs the world over display an aggressive response to post deliveries because they are experiencing the emotion of fear. Every day millions of dogs return to emotional homeostasis after the Posty has gone. Actually, slightly later than that because there is a rebound past the mid point into the smug satisfied feeling of, "That showed 'em!"

How do you stop a dog barking at delivery men and women? Standard method is to yell and maybe give her a slap on the bottom or snout, if she won't shut up.

What emotion is she in? Fear. A negative emotion. Will shouting at her make it better or worse? All those who said, "worse" go to the top of the class. So, will that stop her barking or will it make her more afraid next time? Now she is not only afraid of the intruder into our territory, she is also afraid of the response she will get from us when they arrive! She knows they will probably arrive again tomorrow, but now she is worried that she will be shouted at again. Which makes her anxious. Which pushes her below the point of balance for her emotions (called the point of hedonic balance, but we've done enough Greek lately).

One bad method of training has implications for the emotional equilibrium of our dog. Aeroplanes, shotgun blasts, fireworks and things that she doesn't recognise add to anxiety because she can't hide, run or fight them. None of her normal coping strategies get rid of the problem. She is drifting towards anxiety as a normal state. How easy is it to train an anxious dog? Not very.

Coco was a King Charles Spaniel that had issues with the delivery of post. Jenny, her owner, had been told that if she didn't do something about Coco, she would have to collect her mail from the post office. The post delivery lady was having no more of it!

I was quite surprised that a King Charles Spaniel could be so scary but, when I met Coco at the yard gate of their converted farm, she certainly looked fearsome, baying hysterically at me. Jenny invited me in whilst Coco snapped, snarled and made lunges towards my trouser leg, but without making contact. She was always behind me, darting back and forth with her tail held low. Coco was scared. Over tea and biscuits, some of which found their way from me to Coco, we quietly made friends and after half an hour she was sitting on my knee, having her ears fondled.

Clearly Coco was experiencing a negative emotion when people arrived in the yard and we had to change it. The first thing we did was to provide a secure mailbox attached to the gatepost, so the post delivery lady didn't have to come in the yard, but that was more of a stop-gap than a solution.

Our next purchase was a wire-free door chime kit. We taught Coco that, when the doorbell chimed, she got a biscuit. We moved the door chime all over the house, and, pretty soon Coco was running to the chime for her reward when we operated the remote control. Then we put the wire free door chime inside the secure mailbox and fastened to bell push next to it.

Jenny kept Coco in the house and I left, to return two minutes later and press the bell on the gate. Sure enough, Coco came galloping out, hesitated, barked twice, and then, when I pressed the bell again, came for her biscuit.

240

We were changing the emotion Coco felt towards people coming through the gate.

As luck would have it, there was a family get-together scheduled for the weekend and lots of relatives would be coming to the house. An ideal training opportunity! Jenny spent the evening on the phone explaining that nobody came in without ringing the bell and giving Coco a biscuit. A large Tupperware box of biscuits was placed by the bell.

On Saturday we explained to the post lady what we wanted her to do on Monday, and she was only too happy to oblige.

Two years on, Coco still barks at people who arrive at the gate, but it is a positive emotional "please give me a biscuit" bark rather than the fearful noise she used to make. Jenny quite likes being alerted that someone is there.

On the odd occasion that the post delivers something too big to go in the box on the gate, the post lady is no longer worried about coming in, and Coco positively looks forward to her arrival and, of course, a biscuit.

How do you stop a dog barking at delivery men and women? You change the emotion.

Dogs in emotional deficit find ways to increase their positive emotions. Hence, dogs that are left alone chew things to make themselves feel better. It doesn't stop the loneliness, but chewing is pleasant and the positive balances the negative a little. Dogs that don't get enough exercise to supply their needs may hump the cushions. It doesn't use up *much* energy, but it makes them feel a little better. The whole range of emotions is used to try to push up to the point of balance. Any deficit is countered, at least slightly, by any positive the dog can find to use.

Back to Janet. I never found out why Barney first pooped on the Wilton, but I knew that the anxiety he was feeling made it more likely to continue. Barney spent all day worrying that he was going to be in trouble when Janet came home. Lots of anxiety drove his balance of emotions down. He had little that he could do to improve his overall emotional state, but he knew that pooping made him feel a bit better. Not much, but any help in pushing towards emotional homeostasis was better than none at all. First strategy in the programme to stop Barney pooping was to remove the cause of anxiety: Janet's annoyance. To be fair, as soon as she realised that Barney wasn't capable of feeling guilty, she was overcome with remorse. Second stage was to provide games and toys that increased Barney's emotional equilibrium whilst Janet was not there (see how important toys and games are?) Final stage was some jigging about with feeding times and quantities, but in all honesty, that was really just to break the habit.

How do I know what my own dog's emotional state is? How do I know if she is under stress and unhappy? Well, once we've taken care of the obvious welfare issues like food, water, a place to stay and some games to play, the secret is in predictability and/or control.

Experiments done by giving rats electric shocks (way back in the early 70's) showed that if the rats could either predict the shock, or control it, they suffered less stress than those that were randomly shocked. A little bit of stress is good for us all. It keeps us on our toes and provides for an interesting life. Small challenges to our emotional homeostasis provide us with the opportunity to exercise our minds. Huge challenges or constant confusion cause us stress.

Dogs will suffer stress if they are unable to predict or control their challenges. That is why our relationship is so important. If our dog is constantly threatened by circumstances she can neither predict nor control, she will suffer stress and anxiety, her emotional account will plummet into deficit and she may take to trying all manner of weird and wonderful things to raise it again. Things like barking, chewing the furniture, humping the vicar's leg, wetting the bed, howling at the moon, biting the kids, eating stones, digging up the garden, chasing her tail, coprophagia (look it up, it's not nice), catching imaginary flies, bouncing off the walls, licking herself until it bleeds or running away from home.

"Predict and Control" is why Posty is not a problem, but fireworks are. When fireworks attack they are neither predictable, nor controllable. She never knows when they will strike, or how to get rid of the problem. Anxiety levels rise and emotions plummet. When Posty turns up, very predictably every day, she can control how she feels by chasing the problem away. She only suffers a little anxiety, because she knows exactly how to deal with the situation.

The emotional roller coaster goes:-
Challenge to emotions – dip into anxiety – inherited response of defence aggression - resolution of problem – emotional reward of relief.

Next time the dip into anxiety is not as severe because she knows how to control the problem. However, from her perspective, if it works in these circumstances, it might work for other challenges too. Aggression might become the first choice problem solver. She is using an inherited coping strategy that works for wild canines and the original dog. It is not genetically prepared to deal with the challenges to a pet dog.

With Coco we changed the original emotion so that people arriving were no longer a challenge, but a pleasure. In different circumstances we might change the coping strategy from defence aggression to a more acceptable alternative. Dogs that show aggression towards people they meet in the street can be taught that making eye contact with Mum makes the problem go away. The roller coaster ride would be:-

Challenge to emotions – dip into anxiety – learned response of eye-contact – resolution of problem by Mum – emotional reward of relief. This way our dog has no need to use aggression and we control her behaviour.

Look at your dog's environment. Are you consistent? Can she predict what is going to happen? If not, can she control how she feels by removing the problems? If she can, she is probably an emotionally contented dog. If she can't, you can start applying the secrets for a happy dog.

Joshua using science to train Bonnie not to jump up.
You'll notice that although under some pressure, he never
loses control.

Chapter Eleven
Using Science

There *Are* No Secrets

Now you see you don't need witchery, magic spells, special powers, healing hands, burnt offerings, sacrificial oils, telepathy, astral projections, ectoplasm, metaphysical mutterings, astrology, dowsing, flower power, meditation, voodoo, quackery, crypto-zoology or any of the other weird and wonderful dog training techniques proposed by the myriad of well-meaning "experts" out there.

At this point somebody usually stands up and, in a very loud voice, says something like, "Well, I applied unction of ground chameleon's pancreas to my dog's tail whilst chanting the sacred mantra three times daily, as proposed in the writings of the Blessed Dog-Botherers of Greater Muttering, and she's much better behaved now." And she probably is.

Like any other placebo effect, if they start some kind of programme of actually paying their dog a different kind of attention, there will be a change. She only has two ways to go. She'll either continue to get worse or get better. If she gets worse they abandon the Blessed Dog-Botherers in favour of the next quack. If she improves, the Botherers' list of converts grows.

In fairness, many of these supposed methods at worst don't do any harm and at best pick up some of the scientific principles; they just don't know that they're doing it.

That famously charismatic Grande Dame of 1980's television dog training, Barbara Woodhouse, conformed to the principles, she just didn't explain what she was doing (I doubt she knew). She used control and communication. The dog was in absolutely no doubt what it had to do and that it was offered no other options. That she also used negative reinforcement (applying pressure, then releasing it when the dog performed) was more a product of her time than a lack of expertise.

The problems start when the dog, for whatever reason, responds differently to the trainers' expectations. Because they don't know the background science, they have nothing to fall back on when it isn't going right. I've lost count of the "problem dogs" I've improved by going right back to the basics. The first question to answer is, "What does this dog actually want?" which requires knowledge of ethology (the original dog), genetics (breed specific behaviour), canine behavioural psychology (the emotions) and cognitive theory (what the dog has learned already). When you have those answers you can start to use them to help the dog and owners live a more fulfilling life.

Fashions in dog training come and go as their adherents find that the emperor is actually naked after all, but the vast wealth of scientific research stands minute scrutiny. And that's the reason to use scientific principles to train our dogs: because scientific method means that they *have* undergone minute scrutiny. Rather than the ramblings of one or two people, all the scientists that have contributed to our knowledge labour in the understanding that what they produce will be examined by their peers. And if it *doesn't* pass muster, it will be thrown out.

Most of the Dog-Botherers' methods ultimately rely on, "I've a special understanding that no one else has." Or

"Because I've decided it is like that." Now, faith-based systems are fine as religions, but not for dog training. The scientific approach, whilst acknowledging that the information is only the best discovered up to now, relies on each piece being meticulously scrutinised by other experts, not only in the same field, but also in many related ones. We've seen how many different disciplines contribute to the understanding of dogs. Each one of those depends on how the understanding of it relates to all the others.

It is like pieces of a great big jigsaw, where each piece has its own experts in which way round it goes, and the experts on "bits of sky" know exactly how they fit with "bits of tree", and the "bits of tree" experts know how they fit the "bits of sky" *and* the "bits of haywain".

With the advent of genetic mapping there was a new study that tried to pinpoint the date at which dogs and wolves separated in their ancestry. The methods were very advanced for their time and the research was so good that the results were published in a respected journal. It suggested that dogs and wolves split 100,000 years ago. This was incredible news, pushing back the accepted dates tenfold, and was picked up by the popular press as a breakthrough in our understanding.

What the popular press didn't pick up was the subsequent examination of the study by several other eminent people, which showed why the dates couldn't be true. After some intellectual sparring it is pretty much universally accepted that the true dates are nearer those in chapter one.

If a scientist comes up with something new, there is a whole crowd waiting to test the theory. It would be wrong of me to think that some of them delight in ripping other people's theories apart. Obviously it is all done for the advancement of knowledge and not with any malicious intent. But even if it *was* spiteful, it would still be effective.

The facts have been checked, time and time again, against the best information available, by the best people in their field. There's nothing about a geneticist that makes them better able to train dogs than you or I, or about a neurologist that gives them a special relationship with their dogs. But they are all incredibly specialised in their fields, which gives them sight of a small but extraordinarily detailed part of the big picture that is as perfect as it can be. We all benefit from their expertise by taking from it the parts pertaining to dog owning. I'm not clever enough to appreciate the finer points of genetics or ethology, or all the other 'ologies, but I can understand enough to pick out the bits I need to train my dog.

251

Science gives us an insight into how dogs tick and, once we understand it, it all works for every dog. No more, "Ah, but you can't teach Salukis that." Or, "German Shepherds don't respond to this kind of training." Age and breed differences might make it more or less difficult, but applying the scientific principles works for all ages, types, breeds and both sexes of dogs. You can even use it to teach an old dog new tricks if you like, or help people understand their pets a little better.

To illustrate this I'm first going to use that very understanding to solve a simple but extremely common pet behaviour problem, then I'll look at what was a really serious problem that was resulting in a breakdown of the dog's relationship with her owners.

"Jumping up" is one of the most common and annoying behaviours that owners complain about. There are various methods that can be used to deal with it, but in changing behaviour we first have to ask what drives it. Why do dogs jump up at us?

Dogs jump up at us for two main reasons. Jumping up and licking at the face is normal puppy greeting behaviour that originally stimulated regurgitation. It is also appeasement behaviour, seen in dogs that want to convey that they are not a threat. In puppies it is an inherited motor pattern. They can't help it, they are literally born to do it. It is pre-programmed in them to display to their mother and any other adult they see that might pose a threat. If we were to translate it into words they would be saying, "Hello, it's great to see you. I want you to know that I mean you no harm. Please don't hurt me." As a puppy motor pattern, if it is not reinforced it will fade away as the dog matures. Which is great when they are communicating with their own species, or someone else who understands them. But what usually happens is that we reinforce it like mad when they are a cute little puppy. We encourage our little ball of fluff to be pleased to see us and enjoy it when they leap about like a demented Tigger.

Then, at about six or eight months of age, our cute little puppy becomes a slobbering menace. Tights are ripped, suits are dirtied, toddlers are knocked flying and visitors are intimidated. "Enough is enough!" we cry, along with "Get Off!" "Get DOWN Shep!" and "That dog needs some training!" So we take some advice.

Let's start with the barbaric advice. This ranges from stepping on their back paws, through kneeing them in the chest, to holding and squeezing their front paws when they jump up. Positive punishment contingent on the behaviour of "jumping up". It may well work, but remember what our dog was trying to say? "Pleased to see you"?

"Please don't hurt me"? And what do we do? Hurt them. How do they feel now when we come in? Scared, worried and frightened to say "hello". We are not only punishing "Jumping up", we're also punishing "greeting" and "appeasement". How does that make them feel about us? They can't greet us, and they can't ask not to be hurt. This could be the beginning of the end of our relationship. And that's only if it works! There are also opportunities to make it worse. The bouncier dogs may see it as an extension of the game and increase their levels of bounciness, sidestepping our feet and rebounding from our knees with glee. Worse, the more reactive dogs may respond to the pain with aggression, almost by reflex. So let's not do that.

Less painful would be the use of the popular TV trainers' "rattle-bottle". A plastic bottle or a soft drinks can with a few pebbles or pennies in it which, when shaken, makes a noise. A few seconds' examination identifies it as an aversive noise stimulus. If it is going to work it will do so by making the dog afraid of the noise, which means they become afraid of plastic bottles and cans in lots of other situations. Good, or not good? The other consideration is that it has the same consequences for our relationship as the pain did. It still makes *us* aversive.

"Ignore them." We are told. Not the, "Just let them do it without reacting," kind of ignoring, but actively taking our attention away. Don't speak, look at, or acknowledge our dog in any way for ten minutes after coming in. Now this isn't *bad* advice. It avoids yelling at them and punishing them with pain and noise. It is still negative punishment (taking away something nice) of the behaviour of jumping up, through the removal of our attention, but more benign than anything else we've considered so far. It is still aversive, but probably less so than pain or noise. The problem is that we're also ignoring the greeting and appeasement. If greeting and appeasement are ignored, the dog's most likely reaction will be to try to greet or appease even more! Which leaves us standing with our backs to our dog, arms folded, grim lipped, looking at the ceiling for ten minutes every time we come in, as our dog tries their, so far successful, greeting bounce all around us. If you leave it like that, and then greet your dog after the ten minutes is up or when they calm down, it might actually work. But it may take forever, because every time you come through the door, your dog is pleased to see you and wants to greet you. The urge for them to do so won't go away.

We can shorten this process by cleverly teaching our dog an alternative way to greet us. If we discourage jumping through removing our attention, they don't know what they *should* do. Providing them with another behaviour that results in the attention coming back again would greatly enhance their understanding. Train our dog to sit, or even better, to sit in a specific place, like on their day-bed. But don't try to do it when they are actually greeting us. Train it when they are calmer, until they are really good at it. Remember the phases of learning? New behaviour is best trained with no distractions whatsoever, so when we're coming in the door is probably the worst time to try to teach an alternative to jumping. When they are really good at sitting on their bed, go out of the front door and immediately come back in again, ask them to sit on their bed and reward.

If they can't cope with that, gradually increase the salience of the stimulus, so that they never get too excited to sit on their bed for a reward. If knocking on the door makes our dog go into a frenzy of expectation so that they ignore everything we say, tap gently on the table and ask them to sit on their bed. Tap on the back of the front door whilst still in the room. Open the door and tap on the outside. Go outside and tap on the door then come in. Hammer on the door from the outside. At every step make sure our dog is able to go sit on their bed for a reward. The last stage would be to go out of the back door, round to the front and knock or use your keys to come in.

This is a brilliant way to train our dog in a new greeting behaviour. Provided no one else lets them jump up. Oops! A flaw in our plan. We've taught our dog not to jump up at us, but they're still jumping up at other people because some other people encourage them. Like a gambler, they're on a partial reinforcement schedule, which actually makes the behaviour more likely, and less resistant to extinction. So we've only *actually* trained our dog not to jump up at *us*.

The biggest part of the jumping up problem is that we can't control other people. There will always be the bloke (it's nearly always a bloke – perhaps because we are less likely to wear tights) who says, "I don't mind, let him jump. Clever dog!" which means we can't generalise the training.

Let's think about this for a moment. We want our dog to be able to greet people, but we don't want them to jump up at everyone. Our dog's greeting behaviour is controlled by all the people they greet, through reinforcing whatever our dog is doing at the time with the attention they get. What we need to be able to do is to place our dog's greeting behaviour under *our* control, then if someone doesn't mind them jumping, we can allow it.

When dogs jump up they think they are greeting, or sometimes appeasing. They often don't even realise that they *are* jumping. It is a genetically pre-programmed motor pattern that switches in when they meet someone. Until they understand that they *are* jumping, they'll think they're being ignored for greeting which, as we've seen, makes the behaviour more persistent. We need to be able to tell them that greeting is fine, but jumping isn't; that if they are asked to jump up, they can do, but not if they're asked not to. We want to be able to do that without causing our dog any confusion and without using punishment. Sounds complicated? It's dead easy.

To stop our dog jumping up, first we have to teach them to jump up. "But they already know how to do that!" I hear you chorus. Yes, but they don't know *that* they are jumping. They think they are greeting. If we put it on command, they will understand what jumping up is. Only then can we ask them to stop.

Take a treat in your hand and stand facing your dog. Pat your knee (ankle, thigh, hip or shoulders depending on their size) and encourage them, "Up!" When they jump up on you, stroke the back of their head, tell them they are clever and deliver the treat into their mouth (using the "Okay" signal for exact reward). Take half a step back without speaking and your dog will drop back onto all fours. Immediately repeat the process. After three or four times, your dog will be jumping on command. If they jump before the command, take an early half step backwards so they do not make contact, then get your command in earlier next time.

After five or six times, do not reward with the treat when your dog jumps up. Tell them they are good and stroke their head, after all, they've done as you asked, but then say, "Off" and immediately take the half step back. As their feet hit the floor, say "Okay" and treat. Repeat this several times and call a halt to your training session.

Next training session only reward a couple of "Up!"s before moving on to "Off"s. During this training you will find it more difficult to get your dog to jump, because the primary reward is beginning to be associated with all four feet on the floor. If you want to shape a "sit" as greeting behaviour, tip the treat back over your dog's head as they stand in front of you and reward when they drop their bum onto the floor.

After several training session over a few days your dog will understand what "Up!" and "Off" mean and start to respond to the words alone. Now get a partner involved as the jumped-upon person. Your partner should give the "Up!" command and praise for jumping, and you give the "Off" command just as they step back. Then your partner rewards with the treat when all four feet hit the floor. You are taking control of your dog's behaviour with other people.

Increase the excitement by getting your partner to go out of the door and come back in again, then give the "Off" command as they come in but before your dog starts to jump. Your partner rewards with attention for keeping all feet on the floor.

Work through the process of increasing excitement but keeping control, and the control stays with you. You decide if your dog jumps or not. If the daft bloke wants your dog to jump up onto him, don't give the "Off" command. If it is anyone else, give the "Off" and ask them to give your dog a pat whilst their feet are on the floor.

Simplicity itself, without punishment, without aversion, without damaging your relationship, without allowing other people to spoil your training, without any kind of spin, accomplished through understanding of the science of dog training. But are more complex problem behaviours as easy to solve? Perhaps not as easy as that, but applying the "dog secrets" of science can make them simple to understand.

When I started seeing problem behaviour cases, one of my first was a Cairn Terrier called Madge. Madge barked. A survey of ordinary pet owners reported that one in sixteen dogs vocalised incessantly and a further one in seven when left alone. Madge barked at everything that moved and lots of things that didn't. Not just at a knock at the door, but at children in the street, noises on the TV, their new kitten, birds on the bird table, rain on the conservatory roof, all visitors, passing dogs, even at her owners if they moved too quickly or unexpectedly.

Adult wolves only bark for one reason: a low "wuff" to convey a danger signal to pups near the den.

Madge's owners, Joyce and Harold, thought she might be barking out of spite, because it coincided with them buying a new kitten. Spite, of course, is an emotion that requires self awareness, so dogs don't do spite, although it might look like they do from an anthropomorphic viewpoint.

When I looked into "barking" as a dog behaviour, I found *eighteen* possible causes. Without the science to fall back on, I couldn't possibly investigate Madge's problem. It was certainly neither wolf nor human behaviour!

It turned out that Madge was frightened of almost everything. She was now three but since they'd first adopted her, as an eight-week-old bundle of fluff, she'd snuggled up to their big old cuddly tabby cat, Matilda. Matilda was getting on in years and didn't mind sharing her cosy bed with Madge. Everything was fine until sadly, one day Matilda passed away. Without her friend to rely on, the bottom dropped out of Madge's world. She wasn't a confident dog and the one dependable thing in her life was taken away. She had used Matilda as a solid base from which to view the world, much as a puppy uses their mum. Matilda didn't react much to anything. Snoozing in bed was her favourite activity and even though Madge was considerably more active, she was able to check in with Matilda to see her reaction to anything, and snuggle up in times of stress. After losing Matilda, Madge needed to be able to adjust and find new strategies to help her cope with life's slings and arrows.

Seeing that Madge was bereft, "she moped about all day, whining", Joyce and Harold thought she needed company so, after a suitable period of mourning for Matilda, they bought a kitten, Tilly.

Madge had never seen a kitten before. Matilda had been fourteen when she had first met her, and was a pretty good impression of Bagpuss. The ten-week-old Tilly terrorised Madge. She was chased and pounced on at every opportunity. Even her comfy old bed, which she had shared with Matilda in the corner of Joyce and Harold's bedroom, had been thrown out and replaced by a brand new one.

Madge just couldn't cope any longer. Everything became a challenge to her emotions. In a permanent condition of heightened anxiety, she kicked off at almost everything, from the phone ringing, to birds flying past the window. Joyce and Harold, at their wits end with the din, resorted to shouting at her, changing her dinner time, moving her bed to the kitchen, taking her to training classes, rattling cans at her, putting her outside and, eventually, blasting her with a high pitched "bark deterrent" aerosol noise can. By now Madge was terrified.

Through an understanding of the principles of canine ethology, communication, emotional homeostasis and behavioural organisation, and the consequences of applying aversive methods, together we were able to work out what was going on. Joyce and Harold were mortified when they realised what they had done, and threw themselves into an anxiety reduction programme. Within a month we had Madge almost back to her old self, and peace once more broke out.

Why had Joyce and Harold got it so wrong? They knew Madge had a special bond with Matilda, so thought she knew about cats, but they didn't realise that she wouldn't be able to cope with the entirely different feline behaviour of a new kitten. Madge was three years old; she had only ever seen an elderly cat before and just couldn't comprehend kitten behaviour, such as when Tilly leapt on her tail whilst she slept.

They didn't understand that Matilda was a major part of what kept Madge emotionally balanced; that she was more attached to Matilda than she was to them. They didn't understand that Madge couldn't feel "spite" because it is an emotion that requires empathy.

They were unable to communicate that they wanted her to stop barking, so spoke louder and louder, in an effort to make themselves understood.

They'd read a book that suggested that she didn't know her place in their pack, so they fed her after they'd had their dinner and moved her bed downstairs to the kitchen, taking the opportunity to replace Matilda's decrepit old one with a more aesthetically pleasant one.

They took her to a dog training class in the village hall, where she'd been so scared when the trainer picked her up and shook her to stop her barking that she bit him. He told them she was dominant, so they rattled a can at her and put her outside, where she barked even more.

Finally they bought an aerosol specially marketed to stop dogs barking that read, "Interrupts unwanted behaviour...(including) unwanted barking". Now she ran away to the farthest corner of the room and barked from under the sideboard.

Joyce and Harold had tried treating her as a human. They'd tried treating her as part of their wolf pack. They'd tried to address her dominance. They'd tried the mumbo-jumbo. They'd tried the recommended gadgets. They'd tried their best. But nobody had told them the real secrets.

To combat Madge's barking, first we recognised her behaviour for what it was: chronic stress because of the removal of one of her maintenance set of major comforts, Matilda, and the introduction of a major challenge, Tilly. This resulted in a stressed response to almost every little trial she faced. A knock at the door isn't frightening, until we are on the edge of our seats engrossed in watching a horror film, when it makes us jump out of our skin!

The same thing was happening to Madge. Permanently on edge, everything spooked her into barking. Barking was Madge's way of expressing her anxiety. "Look out! Danger!" was what she felt and that's exactly what she was communicating. Apparently defeating each challenge (the phone always stops ringing, the postman always goes away, the noisy aerosol always stops eventually) reinforced the strategy through operant conditioning. From Madge's point of view: "I bark at the problem and it goes away. Therefore if I want to a problem to go away, I bark." And almost everything was a problem because she couldn't reach emotional equilibrium, that mid-point in her emotions where she felt okay.

We stopped all punishment and started to reduce anxiety by controlling the three most important things in Madge's life, food, games and especially attention. She quickly learned to sit quietly for her food and we introduced a food ball for her to chase round the kitchen in the morning, so she could earn some of her rations through a predatory game.

We salvaged her old bed from the garage, moved it back into the bedroom and cushioned it with part of an old bed sheet soaked in Joyce and Harold's scent, and a heat-pad for extra comfort. Tilly happily stayed in the new bed in the kitchen.

We taught Madge to sit and look at Harold or Joyce for a piece of sausage, and used that to relax her when she was stressed out. Through Madge calmly sitting and looking at her owners, we were able to break the connection between her barking and the problem going away. She had an alternative problem solving strategy.

In the garden we used terrier specific behaviour to improve her emotions by introducing a bark-pit, like a sand-pit but containing forest bark, where treats were hidden for her to dig up.

Both Harold and Joyce started to play games of fetch and hide and seek with her, increasing the opportunities she had to experience good emotions, associating those emotions with them, and countering the negative feelings that had been associated with them through rattle-cans, exclusions and bark deterrents.

Their most difficult task was ignoring the barking that remained, but they found it much easier to reward her relaxed behaviour with lots of calm attention.

Most fun of all was introducing her to kitten behaviour. Every morning, afternoon and evening, for ten minutes, Madge would sit on Harold's lap on the sofa and Joyce would dangle a toy mouse on a fishing rod at the other end of the room for Tilly to play with. This gave Tilly an outlet for her predatory play behaviour and let Madge watch her from a place of safety and comfort.

Each day, as Madge became more and more relaxed, Tilly's game came closer and closer until, three weeks after we started, Madge jumped off Harold's lap and chased the toy mouse! I won't pretend it was an easy road, but that was the start of a firm friendship, as dog and cat played together, chasing and being chased in turn. Madge had to take some "time-outs" on Harold's lap when Tilly got too much for her, and Tilly had her bed to retreat to when Madge played too roughly, but they began to enjoy each other's company more and more.

As the balance of good emotions overtook the anxiety and stress in Madge's life, the need to bark diminished. These days you hardly hear a peep out of her, other than the half-dozen excited yips when you ring the doorbell.

Harold and Joyce thought that Madge's recovery was magical. For six months they had fought an ever-losing battle with Madge's barking, and within a month we had turned the corner, back to the happy Madge she used to be. But it wasn't magic, just carefully applied knowledge, gleaned from the best scientific sources.

I hope you've understood by now that nothing in dog training is a secret; that there is nobody who owns special knowledge; that there are the people who have taken the trouble to find out the scientific facts about dogs, and there are the rest. I hope that I've persuaded you to go and find out a little bit more about dogs in general, to help you learn more about your own dogs in particular. The more we know, the better our understanding; the better our understanding, the more rewarding our relationship. The more people there are who actually understand their dogs, the fewer dogs have to suffer at the hands of the well-intentioned uninformed. Go on, spread the word. It's not a secret!

You can find further information about David Ryan on his ironically named website at www.dog-secrets.co.uk where you can also buy his book

"Stop!" How to control predatory chasing in dogs

As a police dog handler and instructor I became fascinated by why and what dogs chased. Of course police dogs are supposed to chase, it's how they catch the bad guys, but they do it in a particularly controlled way and only on command.

What follows is the fullest explanation of canine predatory chase behaviour ever written. It answers all the questions, not just for police dogs, but for the misunderstood pets and the confused owners who can't stop them chasing. It also contains the most complete behaviour modification programme for avid chasers but, before we get to that, we need to get inside the canine psyche to understand what exactly predatory chasing is...